D1563176

Ephesians 3
Verses 17- 21

And I pray that Christ will be more and more at home in your hearts as you trust in Him. May your roots go down deep into the soil of God's marvelous love.

And may you have the power to understand, as all God's people should, how wide, how long, how high, and how deep His love really is.

May you experience the love of Christ, though it is so great you will never fully understand it. Then you will be filled with the fullness of life and power that comes from God.

Now glory be to God! By His mighty power at work within us, He is able to accomplish infinitely more than we would ever dare to ask or hope.

May He be given glory in the church and in Christ Jesus forever and ever through endless ages. Amen.

iii

Editor: Jodi Barrows, Linda Watts

Additional Editing: Jenny Singleton, Martha Fitch

ISBN-13: 978-0-9766858-4-5
ISBN-10: 0-9766858-4-1

1st Printing

SNS PUBLISHING

Our Family Line

Moses Gimlin Austin Gimlin
7.22.1858   8.14.1818

Harris/Tate
Married 6.5.1898

Pa & Granny
Gimlin

Izell Thomas

Mineola Tate

Izell   Lillie
Mineola Tate Thomas

5 Generations of Women

Introduction

I have always enjoyed history of any kind. As a young girl, my sisters and I were told stories about the women in our family. They were exciting and true!

The unique part about our family history is that it all revolves around women! The women all lived to be very old keeping their minds and bodies intact. The youngest died at 82 and the oldest is still alive at 101 living in west Texas! Many times we heard the story from the original lady that lived it. That made the stories so pure and rich. Now, the other thing about these females is that many were widows at a very young age of 18 to 32. Also, for five generations every child born in each of these marriages was female.

These women and their lives are the base of the story for the Maillys in my books. The family will continue for over 150 years in over a dozen books or more. I hope you enjoy these stories as much as my sisters and I did growing up.

Oh, one more thing, my sisters and I have all broken the chain by not being widowed young and we have male children.

I have included some great photo's and I would like to tell you about some of them.

The first photo is Moses Gimlin on the left with his father, Austin. Austin was born in 1818 and had 3 sons and 3 daughters. I can't believe I have a family photo from a man born almost two hundred years ago! My mother's dad was a Gimlin.

In our story, Grandpa Lucas as a widower, raised a family of females. He never remarries when his wife Claire dies. This is similar with Moses Gimlin. He had 10 children, the oldest a boy, William Edgar Gimlin. The others were girls, 9 of them. He raised a house full of females alone. Moses was married to Nora Wheeler. They lived in south Oklahoma in the mid-1860's. Moses lived to be in his 80's and was still alive when my mother was young.

Top right: Emma and Jack Harris. Emma was a sister to my great grandmother, Mineola Tate-Thomas. Jack's siblings had some famous sons that you might remember, Frank and Jessie James. You will hear more on this later.

Middle left: Pa & Granny Gimlin. Pa is Moses' oldest child and only son, William Edgar Gimlin. Leola is granny and was 3/4 Cherokee Indian. She had two sons, Leslie, my grandfather, and Leon. Shortly after she was widowed she accidently died in a house fire after catching her nightgown on fire.

Granny is our "Claire" in the Mailly story. Granny made over 200 quilts in late 1800s. We still have several of them, but most were lost in the fire with her. You will see many of Granny's designs in our quilts in the story. In fact, the "Fire" quilt, a beautiful applique design, will be mentioned in each book. You will get the design at the end of the series. Granny was a hard worker, stubborn and loved to dance. She practiced much of her Indian culture. Granny was an avid gardener and put up hundreds of fruits and vegetable jars in her lifetime. She loved to give of her time and talent.

Back to Edgar, Pa, for a little more info. He was a well-to-do, hard working cotton farmer. A disgruntled "friend" was upset with him and set Edgar's barn on fire. There were horses, a prize sow with piglets, hay and cotton inside the barn. The fire was huge! People from far away saw the blaze and came to help. But, it was too late, all was lost. They lived in the north Texas area of McKinney.

The baby picture is a boy, Izell Thomas, who was married to Mineola Tate, my great grandmother. He died young from a diabetic coma. Izell had been to a church taffy pull on Valentine's Day. He left a pregnant wife, Mineola and a 2 year old daughter Lillie.

Bottom left: Mineola Tate-Thomas, my great grandmother. She was married to Izell thomas (the baby picture above) and widowed at 18, pregnant with my grandmother. She had a 2-year old daughter, my great aunt Lillie.

Ma, Mineola, ran an all female harvest crew of cotton pickers throughout southern Oklahoma and north Texas. When she wasn't working the harvest, she lived with her sister, Emma Harris and her family. Remember Emma and her husband, Jack, had those nephews Frank and Jessie James. This is where the stories of Frank and Jessie come into play. There are so many stories of Mineola's life that are great. But the one where her late husband's photo, which she wore next to her heart, crumbled in her hands is my favorite. This was a great love story. One that could definitely stand the test of time. I remember her well; she passed away when my oldest boy was 9 months old. You will hear a lot more from this great lady's life!

Bottom right: Ma, Mineola, with her two daughters whom she raised alone. My grandmother, Izell, was named after the father she never met. My Great-aunt Lillie passed away December 2000 at age 94. The last time I saw Lillie in south Oklahoma she sat on her porch with several family members. Her legs were in her chair under her like a teenager. We had brought my future daughter-in-law to meet her. She was a great lady!

Mineola's mother was Elizabeth Jane Simons, and her mother was Mary Jane Scarbrough. It was this side of the family that lived in Louisiana. Elizabeth Jane was married twice like our "Liz" and it was her husband that owned the timber mill.

It was also through this branch of the family that the 5 generations of all female children came from. This went from me to my mother, her mother, etc.

This group of ladies were a huge part of my growing up. I spent many privileged years with them. They have stories that make you laugh and cry. These are the women that bring the Mailly women to life.

The next page of photos show the generations of females.

Top left: My mother with her 4th new born daughter and her little niece.

Top right: Two of my girl cousins and one sister.

Middle left: Five girl cousins on Easter at my grandmother's. I am the little one in the front. Two of my sisters are also in the photo. Watch for the famous matching dresses we always wore.

Middle right: My niece. She is taking a quick dip in a 5 gallon bucket on my mother's deck in southwest Kansas. Notice her dog on duty with shoes, towel and panties.

Bottom: My mother with two of her sisters and her mother.

In conclusion: During the decade of the 1850's, the population of Tarrant County grew dramatically. In 1850, a census showed 599 whites and 65 slaves. By 1860, it was 5170 whites and 850 slaves. Even though Fort Worth was abandoned as a military outpost, settlers remained. Old fort buildings were turned into a general store, doctor's office, hotel and dress shop.

Grapevine and Grand Prairie were the fastest growing areas. Birdville was the county seat. The decision was soon questioned by influential citizens of Fort Worth. A special election in 1856 gave Fort Worth the win by a narrow margin. It caused much ill will between the two towns. Finally in 1860, it was permanent with Fort Worth.

On a quilting note, I thought this fact was interesting. With the prelude of war, cotton calico went to $4.00 a yard.

Mailly Family Tree

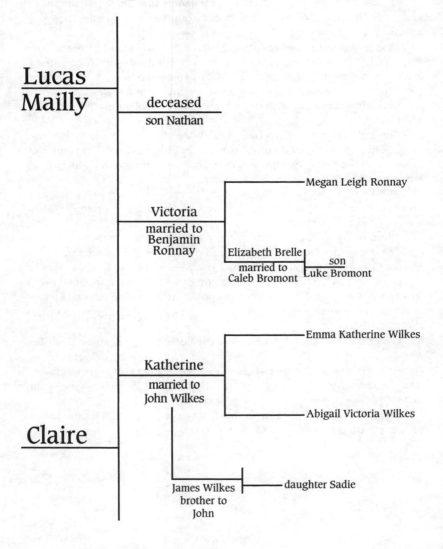

Lucas
Mailly

deceased
son Nathan

Victoria
married to
Benjamin
Ronnay

— Megan Leigh Ronnay

Elizabeth Brelle
married to
Caleb Bromont

son
Luke Bromont

Katherine
married to
John Wilkes

— Emma Katherine Wilkes

— Abigail Victoria Wilkes

Claire

James Wilkes
brother to
John

— daughter Sadie

Chapter One

The Deal

Fort Worth, Texas 1856

North Texas was a beautiful place on this day. The earth rolled gently with the thick grass. Oak trees were scattered along the small hills. The late summer sun was now high in the sky as the eight expectant wagons rolled along the trail. Rainfall had been plentiful this year and the earth rejoiced in it. A small herd of deer grazed silently under a gathering of trees. Each tree was shaped in a uniform half circle. The branches had grown straight out from the trunk to look like they were floating on a layer of air. Not a single twig or branch was out of place. The leaves were layered neatly to produce an abundance of shade to the earth that supported it.

Elizabeth Bromont looked about the countryside and admired its splendor. She knew well the storms that produced the moisture required to sustain the beauty she admired. Yes! She could love this country. It felt like home already.

She gazed across the horizon that would soon be home. Liz breathed in a long breath and bit the side of her lip. Some golden strands of hair had escaped the thick braid down her back and the edges of her bonnet. As she captured her locks of hair and tucked them away, she thought about the man sitting on the wagon bench next to her.

Thomas Bratcher was a hard worker, always treating everyone fairly and with respect. Elizabeth's grandfather, Lucas Mailly, put his trust in Thomas. He expected Thomas to get the family safely to Texas. Not to mention that her son Luke thought Thomas was grand. Thomas and Caleb, her late husband, had been best friends since childhood. She was not sure how old he was, but assumed Thomas was her husband's age. He was a prayerful and patient man.

"How old are you?" she asked.

"What?" Thomas asked, awakened from his own thoughts.

"Thomas, are you my friend?"

Thomas loosely held the wagon reins in his hand so they interloped between his fingers. A smile formed under his new mustache.

"Why all of these questions?" Thomas chuckled. "I knew you were quiet way too long."

Liz was looking into Thomas' eyes, searching to find out if he really was who he seemed to be.

"I have been your friend for many years, you know that."

As Thomas sat, driving the wagon, he was amazed by this woman who had held his interest for so many years. Before Caleb's death, he had really only known her from afar. He had never sat alone with her in a porch swing and listened to her thoughts. He had only watched. This wagon ride was the longest time that he had been alone with Caleb Bromont's widow.

"Liz, I would like to talk to you about something."

Liz looked at Thomas.

"Now that we are almost there, I would like to tell you about the plans your grandfather and I have discussed. You may already know some of them."

Thomas took a breath and continued on as Liz watched him.

"Lucas and I want to start a freight company to bring supplies in for the mercantile. Lucas most likely has a wagon on the way already." Thomas chuckled as he thought of his mentor and friend. Lucas Mailly had the strength and drive of a young man, yet the wisdom of Solomon himself. Lucas could ask Thomas to move the earth the other direction and he would do it. Thomas had never respected and loved a man like he did his boss.

Liz looked at Thomas with her blue eyes and drew his thoughts back to the present.

"Chet, Blue and John want to be freight drivers. We would be the first to bring supplies now that the military has moved on. I want to eventually start a ranch. I think this area has a good chance of being a hub for the cattle business. Lucas and I will be business partners and Luke will grow up to be a part of it also. I feel I'm already a part of this family. I would like to make it official by you marrying me."

Liz kept looking at Thomas. She wasn't sure this was a real proposal. Where was the part about I love you and can't live without you? Did she miss that?

The wheels of the wagon continued round and round as did her thoughts. She took marriage very seriously and would not even consider it without lengthy thought.

Thomas thought she looked puzzled.

"Elizabeth Bromont, I have loved you since the day I saw you on the porch when Lucas was about to give Caleb and me the jobs we came asking for at the timber mill. You stepped out of the door and stood next to the pillar holding your cat. Your hair looked like spun gold in the sun, just as it does today. I knew then you were the one and only for me."

Thomas ran his hand down her braid and watched it in the sun. He turned his hand over to hold her hand in his.

"I was stunned by you. I waited for you to acknowledge me then and now. Because I waited over fifteen years ago, I lost you and I don't want that to happen now. I wanted to court you months ago, but you were grieving over Caleb's death. It just wasn't right; he was my best friend."

Thomas paused and looked ahead.

"Liz, I want to marry you. I don't want to wait any longer or run the risk of losing you again. Luke needs me and even loves me. You will too if you just give us a chance."

Thomas was holding her hand firmly and searching her face for the answer that he wanted.

Liz continued to listen to his confession and was amazed that he had always felt this way; she had never known.

"How could I have not known this?" she thought.

She had wondered why he never married. He was never interested in the girls she tried to place him with so many times.

"I never knew," she said softly and mostly to herself.

"Did Caleb?" she asked, "did he ever know?"

Her head was swimming with memories. She had always felt that Thomas was family. Nothing had ever been out of place or strange.

"No, I don't think so. I never told him. I did a good job of keeping it from everyone except your grandfather," Thomas smiled.

"That man keeps track of his granddaughters like a hawk." Thomas squeezed her hand a little and chuckled.

"Does he know your intentions now?" She looked at him seriously.

"I don't think he would have sent me with you if he had not been in favor of it, Liz."

Thomas thought Liz was a little shaken with his confession and proposal. Maybe he should have waited. She was always a thinker about her decisions. He did know that about her.

"I had a brother in Caleb. I would not have hurt him. Liz, I almost died trying to save him at the mill that day. We were best friends since the first day we met. I think that he would approve of us together and he

4

knew that Luke and I had a special bond. I was always family even when Caleb was alive."

"It must have been hard for you all those years watching us. I'm sorry." She paused and looked at Thomas. "I love Caleb."

"I know you do, Liz. I think you always will and I can take it. I already have. But he is gone and I am here. If you can love me half as much as you loved Caleb, I will die a happy man," Thomas implored.

The wheels of the wagon continued along the grassy trail as they got closer to their destination. Liz watched the scenery pass but none of the beauty registered as it had before. Thomas let her sit quietly and think about all he had said to her. Her hand was still in his.

After several minutes she turned to look at him and thought, "Was he a man that she could love? Share her thoughts and dreams with forever?"

Thomas looked over and bent down to kiss her.

It had been over a year since she had been kissed and it felt good. It was warm, sweet and gentle.

"Thomas, I accept your offer of courtship with the intent to marry with one stipulation. I need you to understand that I will always love Caleb; he is part of me. I do understand that I need to move on. I would like to do that with you." She took a deep breath. "I think I am ready, is it a deal?"

Thomas smiled, took her hand, kissed the back of it and said, "Deal."

Liz looked straight ahead as their destination came closer.

Thomas gave a quick slap of the reins to the team and smiled at his future bride. This was a great new beginning.

Chapter Two
Fort Worth

Liz and the other seven wagons filled with her cousins and supplies traveled the path in single file. The lead wagon was driven by Colt, the youngest Texas Ranger. On the first night that they had met he had scared her to death. He had come into the camp looking like trouble. He was wild and unannounced. Several guns were at his side and his unruly hair was covering his badge. Colt was now their scout. Liz had desperately needed one on this trip. She still was not sure if she would really trust a scout after the first one had gotten them lost as they began their journey. Her experience with this profession was unreliable.

Colt slowed his wagon and each one rolled up next to his. They were stopped on the top of a hill where they could see far into the distance. All they saw was a thick grove of trees with a few old wooden buildings.

"Fort Worth." Tex stated. "We've made it without Indians, stampedes or outlaws."

Tex, the Captain of the Rangers, nodded his head at the two lawmen who rode with him. The Captain was medium height with a slim build. He was old enough to be the women's father. Tex was a legend throughout the territory. His curly brown hair was cut short under his sweat-stained cowboy hat. His tanned, leathery skin reflected the years of riding under the Texas sun.

Jackson and Colt, the other two Rangers who rode with Tex, slapped the reins and clicked their teams to move on.

Liz was thankful that she was without the dangers Tex spoke about. She was not sure that she could have handled any more misfortune. The hardships they experienced had been difficult. Liz discovered that she possessed a full measure of perseverance and her faith continued to be strong. Now that the trouble was behind her she took pride in her ability. She placed all of the accomplishments in her mind as a living stone. She could return to this experience and gain strength from it.

"I can do all things in Christ's power. Philippians 4:13," she recalled.

Her mind quickly returned to the frightening night when she stood holding several teams of horses during a tornado. Rain and lighting dashed about. With each bolt of light you could see the twister dancing toward them. The hail stones repeatedly beat down upon her as she tried to calm the animals and herself. The ragged-edged ice pounded them to a bloody existence. It was about all she could take. She reminded herself that most people quit when the battle is almost won. Perseverance is a trait most individuals never know they have.

It had been her responsibility to keep the group calm and moving toward their goal. She would not disappoint her grandfather.

The wheel of the wagon jolted Liz from her past.

As she looked at the grove of trees and the little wooden structures, she was disappointed in Fort Worth. Her eyes were taking in the view and she could not believe it. She knew that Grandpa Lucas would be very disappointed in this haggard-looking settlement.

The wagons drove into the quiet, abandoned little town. It was not like Lecompte at all. There was not any hustle or bustle or business going on.

Liz was a little confused and saddened by it all.

"Was this a trick? Was Grandpa aware of what this place was like? How could they ever make a living here?" Liz questioned.

She didn't even see a town dog.

Liz looked at Thomas.

"Are you sure this is the right place? Surely we missed it somewhere."

About that time a rider appeared from the trees and rode toward them. He whipped the reins back and forth on the flanks of his mount.

"You're here!" the rider exclaimed as the dirt kicked up behind the pony. He pulled back on the leather bridle as he reached them. With a huge toothless grin he greeted them.

In the wagon behind Liz, rode Megan and Jackson.

Megan was younger than her sister Liz by four years. Her dark hair, smooth skin and green eyes were a beautiful contrast. Everyone that met Meggy agreed that she was quick witted and talented as well.

Jackson was the other Texas Ranger who rode with Tex and Colt. He was tall and broad with a handlebar mustache and a gentle spirit. Jackson won most of his battles by sheer intimidation. Jackson and his black stallion, Zeus, created myth and legend everywhere they went. Zeus patiently trotted along the side of Megan's wagon under Jackson's watchful eye.

Megan whispered to Jackson who had driven with her the last two days. Jackson laughed as Megan said, "it's worse than we thought. He hasn't seen a human in years."

"You must be the Mailly family. Are you Lucas?" The toothless rider looked over to Tex.

"No, I'm Captain Tex of the Texas Rangers, hired to bring this train safely to Fort Worth. Who is in charge here? Can you take us to them, right away?"

"Yeah, sure. They are all at the fort, this way." The rider started west and motioned them to follow.

"What do you call this place?" Liz called out to the rider.

He was too far away to hear Liz so Tex answered her.

"The old outpost before they built the fort. Did you think this was it?"

Tex and the other Rangers laughed as they realized the women thought the outpost was their new home.

Liz let out a sigh of relief as she passed the shabby, splintered buildings and the real fort with life came into view.

"Liz, did you really think that was where we were going to start up?" Thomas quizzed her with a smile.

"Yes and it is not amusing! I was really concerned for a moment."

She smiled when she saw a little church with white double doors and a steeple on top.

Two people were standing out front on the small steps, waving.

"I think that is Pastor Parker and his wife Anna," Liz stated with child-like excitement. "Oh, Thomas this is really happening; they are here waiting for us!"

A few town people began to come from several directions to greet them. They were friendly and anxious to help get them settled in their new home.

"I'm Anna Parker; welcome to Fort Worth. We are so excited to have you here!"

The four Mailly granddaughters gathered close to Anna and introduced themselves. She gave them a hug as she welcomed each one.

"Please don't be too overwhelmed by our excitement of your arrival. We are just anxious to get our little community up and going again. It has been quite concerning with the fort post moving on west. You and your commitments represent life to our town and we are thankful to you," Anna explained.

Liz and the other women knew they were welcomed in the area but had not realized fully that they were to be the new life for the town.

Anna began to lead them in the direction of their new buildings and explained a little more to them as they walked down the boarded sidewalks of Fort Worth, Texas. A small group of citizens followed and listened to every word.

"This is the place where we kept our supplies and these three buildings are yours for the mercantile and Megan's sewing business. They are all yours to do with as you wish. Also, the captain's quarters have the best living conditions. You can call them home."

Anna paused to let her words soak in. She searched each face looking for their thoughts.

Liz was scared but excited. Her mercantile was standing before her. She could see it with her mind's eye and visualize shelves with an abundance of supplies. Yard goods, threads, lace and buttons lay in the center. On the back wall, sugar, coffee, beans and hard tack. Small red check curtains hung at the windows and two double doors with a fresh coat of red paint swung open with warm greetings to every customer. Over the porch, the sign read "Mailly Mercantile." Rocking chairs set out front.

Liz came out of her thoughts as she heard Anna's voice again.

"We would like to have all of you for supper tonight. I will have some sandwiches sent over for you so you can get started right away on settling in. I am so glad to have you here safely. We've planned a Texas cookout for you and will get word out for Sunday. Parker will introduce you to the families of Fort Worth!"

Anna was as sweet as they had all hoped for. She had a soft, soothing voice and her dark hair was very curly. It was pulled up away from her face with a gold hair comb. It fell loosely down her back in a storm of curls.

Liz thought Anna was about Abby's age but not as tall.

"Anna, Abby is my cousin from Mississippi; she is the new teacher Pastor Parker has hired." Liz placed her hand on Anna's arm.

"Oh! In my excitement, I completely forgot about the school. I'm sure the school board members would like to show you the classroom area. My husband is out on a call. Do you mind waiting for Parker to arrive?" Anna asked.

Abby was glad to see all of the emotion about the school. They were definitely wanted in this little town.

"We have plenty to do. I can wait," Abby replied.

"I will send him over as soon as he returns. This is so exciting. I have waited forever to have more women here." Anna reached right over and gave Abby a hug. When she finally released the new school marm, the men were ready to start unloading the wagons, dusty from the Louisiana trail.

"This is Smithy," Anna stated. "He will have these fine gentlemen get you unloaded. Just direct them."

Anna waved goodbye and walked back down the street from where she came.

John turned to Blue with a smile and said, "Oh, Liz can direct you all right."

These two had worked at the Mailly timber mill for years. They now had the chance to move West with the family. John and Blue both respected Lucas and Thomas and would continue their employment.

"Well, we aren't in Louisiana any more." Liz thought as she looked about from the wooden steps in front of the new location for her mercantile.

There was a dirt road out front that disappeared in both directions. On each side of the mercantile were wooden buildings left behind by the Cavalry. A huge pecan tree with its branches reaching twenty feet or more in each direction was across from where she stood. Playing in the nice grassy area beneath the tree were two squirrels surveying the new group of citizens. The church and the new schoolroom were on down from the pecan tree. On the same side of the street where Liz stood, and down to the right, was the smithy. Next to the smithy was a set of corrals, which held two mules and one stallion with a long black mane. He pawed at the edge of the gate and shook his head. His mane hung in the air and demanded attention.

At the end of her boardwalk and back to the left, the street turned and there was where the captain's housing was located. She stepped to the end of the sidewalk to get a better look. She turned to walk a few steps and saw a lovely house with grass, trees and a garden. It was already growing and heavy with a harvest of fresh vegetables. She was quite surprised and turned to tell the others.

She found the group right behind her. They had followed, waiting for her to give the approval that Fort Worth was acceptable and that they would be staying after all.

"Oh," Liz stated. "I didn't realize you were all right with me. Did you see the garden?"

"Mrs. Bromont." A tall handsome stranger stepped from the crowd. "Samuel Smith, Ma'am."

"This was the man standing with Anna Parker when they pulled into the fort," Liz thought.

Everything was happening so fast. She had not been introduced to many of the strangers now standing and looking at her. She reached her hand out, remembering her manners.

"Please excuse me, Mr. Smith. I was lost in thought and…"

He took her hand lightly and smiled a breath-taking grin. She had never heard a voice as smooth and warm as that of Samuel Smith.

Liz seemed to melt as he held her hand.

Samuel never took his eyes away from hers as he continued to speak.

"That is certainly fine. The captain's wife liked a garden and hoped you would tend to it in her absence. She did not move on to the west with her husband. Just a little farther west and it starts to get a little desolate with wind, snakes, and short trees if you're lucky. The weather is more short tempered than any woman I've ever met. Anyway, she went back East."

"Of course, it's an unexpected treasure. Please thank her for me, if you have the opportunity."

Thomas had gone inside the building that would be the mercantile. He had a wagonload of gold that belonged to his employer, Lucas Mailly. He was searching for a place to hide the nest egg. He glanced around for a bank or vault, but did not find one. Just a jail building at the end of the street and that would not work at all. He finally decided that he could go under the floorboards in the mercantile. He would bunk upstairs and could keep an eye on it without anyone knowing.

Thomas walked back to the doorway to look for Liz and the others. He could hear them around to the left and walked toward the sound. What he saw was enough to make him feel protective of what he thought was now his property. A handsome man was holding Liz's hand and smiling at her. Liz seemed to be in a trance.

Thomas' boots walked heavy on the boards and kept beat with his pulse as he advanced to the group. This feeling was new to him. He was not a man quick to anger.

"Thomas, there you are." Liz turned to include Thomas.

"This is Mr. Samuel Smith."

Samuel looked at Thomas who stared firmly at him. Samuel Smith was a smart man and had seen a jealous husband before. He maneuvered around the situation at hand.

"Mr. Bromont, nice to meet you. I was just telling your lovely wife that she could take over the garden."

"Oh, I'm sorry, Mr. Smith, I'm Elizabeth Bromont and this is Thomas Bratcher. He works for my grandfather, Lucas Mailly."

Thomas moved his glare from Samuel to Liz.

She did not know what Thomas was upset about. Liz felt uncomfortable under his stare and continued the introduction.

"This is my sister Megan and my cousins, Abby and Emma Wilkes."

Tex and the others were standing close watching the exchange. Tex did not know what had transpired between Liz and Thomas but he knew that Thomas was not happy with Samuel and even more upset with Liz and that introduction.

"Well, Mrs. Bromont, maybe you could direct us and we will get these wagons unloaded for you," Samuel stated.

Tex saw the opportunity to step in and prevent any more friction. He directed Thomas to the wagon filled with gold.

"Thomas let's get your wagon unloaded first. Jackson! Colt!" Tex called out and the four walked to the wagon full of Mr. Mailly's gold.

Thomas went to work but watched over his shoulder the whole time they secured the gold under the stairs. He was keeping an eye out for two treasures, the gold and the widow Bromont.

Anna soon appeared with cool water and sandwiches. Thomas took two of each and went to eat with Liz.

Liz never liked things to be left hanging and went straight to the point when Thomas handed her the lunch.

"Thomas, I don't know what upset you, but you need to be pleasant to our new friends."

Thomas stood with one leg on the step above him and his back against the porch post of the mercantile.

"What upset me was Mr. Smith's hand holding and your introduction. Is that all I am? A worker for Lucas?"

Thomas held his sandwich without a bite being taken and looked at Liz as she sat on the steps in front of the mercantile. She looked up at Thomas and realized she had hurt his pride.

"Thomas, I'm sorry. I was caught off guard with it all and he was just there. I didn't mean to hurt you."

Thomas was not ready to smooth this over and pressed her for more.

"Why didn't you tell him that we are to be married?"

"Well. I forgot." Liz answered quietly.

"Forgot! How do you forget that?" Thomas was angry but kept his voice low.

Liz was now upset and standing to face Thomas.

"I haven't even told Megan," she firmly stated.

Liz took a breath and looked away for a moment to calm her emotions. Then she began again.

"Thomas, so much has happened today. Please don't be angry with me. Give me a little time to warm up to the idea of marriage."

"I don't know what there is to warm up to!" Thomas took a bite finally and looked away to the group at the wagons.

"You didn't even say I was a family friend," Thomas added.

Calming some, he decided to take a different approach.

"Liz, you have to be careful here. This is not Lecompte and we don't know who we can trust yet. Who is Samuel anyway?"

Liz looked to the group laughing at something Mr. Smith said.

"He knew the fort captain and his wife; I assumed he was a friend. He was with Anna Parker when we arrived."

"Until we know for sure, let's be on the safe side," Thomas warned.

Then he asked, "What do we have left to do?"

"We are ready for the stock to be brought in and placed on the shelves. It was in good shape, just needed some sweeping out. I wish I had some glass windows to be placed in the front, like we had back home. But until we can get it, can we put two doors in the front; it will be nice to see out when the store is open."

"I think I can manage it. I will get Jackson to help."

"If you will have your personal belongings brought upstairs, I will get your things put up, the room cleaned and arranged for you." Liz offered.

"Thomas, I didn't even ask if you wanted the room upstairs."

"That would be good. Do you want your things at the little house with the garden?" he teased.

"Yes, please." She smiled. It felt good to be on peaceful terms with Thomas again.

Thomas took her hand.

"Liz, I'm sorry I was mad, I just don't like sharing you now that I don't have to." Thomas kissed her hand and walked back to the wagons for his tools.

Megan had been watching Liz and Thomas during lunch and didn't disturb them but she was anxious to talk with her sister.

As she walked toward Liz, she passed Thomas and said. "Hey, Thomas did Liz…"

"Yes Megan, she said yes and we are to be married as soon as possible."

Thomas never stopped walking as they passed each other. He had also solved the problem of Liz finding time to tell her sister the news.

Megan was stunned. She watched Thomas as he walked on and then turned to her sister.

"Liz? Is everything alright?"

Megan thought she would side step what was on her sister's mind, for the moment, anyway.

"I'm fine. Thomas and I just …well…were confused."

Liz wanted to move the thought pattern to the chores at hand.

"Megan, what do you think? It's not the comforts of home but it could be worse."

Megan would not turn loose of the topic. She wanted to know what was going on with her sister.

"Liz, tell me what Thomas said to you. He was strange over there with Mr. Smith when we first arrived and now when we were eating the two of you were having an intense conversation."

"I'm just tired and it's been a long day. My emotions have been up and down. Thomas was upset with me. He said we need to be more cautious in this new place."

"Is that all Thomas said? It looked serious at lunch and you didn't join the rest of us."

Liz looked to her sister, not sure how to say it.

"Well," she hesitated, "Thomas wants to marry me."

Megan was as confused as her sister. Finally, Thomas asked her and she agreed, but Liz was not as happy as she should be.

"When did this happen? You don't seem too excited." Megan softly pushed for more details.

"This morning when we were riding in the wagon; it just happened. I told him I loved Caleb and he said that he knew that and it was fine. He is going into business with Grandpa Lucas and ...and that he has loved me since he came to the Riverton Mill all those years ago."

Liz paused with disbelief as she went over it again.

"Megan, he has waited all these years for me."

Megan gave her sister a hug and told her the truth.

"Thomas is a good man and he loves you more than you know. Give him a chance Liz, you won't be sorry. It will be good, you wait and see."

Liz listened to her younger sister and wanted her to be right. She would try, really try.

"I am going upstairs to get Thomas moved in." Liz said. "Can you sweet talk any of those men to get the rest of our things to the house?"

Megan smiled at her sister. She would never have trouble getting help with that. She could always find help with any chore.

Liz continued on with her mental check list of getting settled.

"Megan, the house looked fairly clean. We need some wood chopped and see if you can find out about the water supply and how we get it to us."

Megan chuckled again at her sister asking if she knew how to get help out of any of the men. She also smiled over Liz always giving orders and getting things organized to suit her. Liz usually handled problems by tackling a large workload that would keep her mind off the situation she was dealing with.

"We won't ever be without help Liz. We are the only white single women in the territory. But I did hear Blue tell one of the cowboys that we have a bite."

Both women laughed and walked up the steps together. They stood on a wooden boardwalk that would become a very familiar location to them.

"Tex said at lunch that we should make it a habit of carrying our guns." Megan said.

"Does he think we don't just because he can't see them?" Liz asked.

"Maybe," Megan said, "I like him…he…well, he is like a dad. Liz, I don't remember our father."

Liz stopped and looked at her younger sister.

"He was a good man. He loved us a lot. He called you his wildflower. You were a feisty, little thing then, too."

Megan smiled as her sister talked. She still couldn't remember him.

"I will be to the house when I finish with the upstairs."

Liz gave her sister a wink as she turned to walk into her new shop and up the back staircase to Thomas' living quarters.

Chapter Three
Thomas' Log Cabin

Liz entered a nice size room above the mercantile. The stairs to the living quarters were at the end of the building with easy access to a back door that went across to the main house where the Mailly women would live. From the windows, Thomas would have a full view of the house and that would make Liz feel more secure. The upstairs was furnished quite nicely with a good bed, washstand and a chest of drawers. One lamp was left on a table with several books on the bottom shelf and a rocking chair. She dusted everything well and opened the crates that had been brought up with the belongings of the man she was to marry.

It was a strange feeling. She took out his clothing and shook them out to air. As she inspected them, she found that they were all in good shape. She could not find any that needed mending. In fact they all looked almost new. She refolded and placed them in the chest of drawers and on a few pegs that lined one wall by the washstand.

The next crate had a family Bible that was well worn. She opened the cover and saw the family names written on the inside page. She found

Thomas William Bratcher, the third son to Susan and William Bratcher written on the faded, worn page. Liz discovered that one son had died of infection at age three. The oldest was still living. She had met him once at the mill.

Then she saw it, a beautiful log cabin quilt. It was so different; it had triangles going around the outside of four cabin blocks that had been sewn together. Liz quickly fluffed the mattress of straw and placed the clean sheets on the bed. She then took the quilt from the box and smoothed it over the bed. The colors of the quilt were stunning with brown and cream colored logs matching up to the deep red triangles that surrounded the cabins. This pattern made a large block and Liz could hardly take her eyes from it. As she ran her hand across it, admiring the stitches, she saw a letter that had fallen from the quilt when she unfolded it. As she picked it up, a page fell open.

His mother wrote, *"Thomas, we miss you so much and wish you would come closer to home, especially now that Caleb has passed. Your father and I know how close you were and we are saddened for you. I hope you enjoy the quilt I made for you. The log cabin blocks represent your life of working with the logs at the mill and the longing for a home of your own. You would be a great father and husband. The red center of each cabin is the love you have for the woman who won't or can't return it. Somehow you have kept that love alive in your heart. She must be very special. The red triangles or claws are the troubles we all have finding our own home and happiness. Thomas, please don't be upset for me speaking my mind and caring about my youngest son. I just love you and want you to be happy. Please consider coming back home. We have many fine young women who would be honored to be your wife and would make you a loving home. I have prayed for you endlessly as I worked on this quilt. I hope you can feel your mother's love and my desire for you to be happy. I trust that this quilt will bring you what you wish. Love always, your Mother."*

Liz now sat in the rocker that was by the lamp and thought about what she had just read.

"Thomas had loved her for years and she didn't even know it. He waited for her. He was now excited about marriage; he had plenty of time to get ready for it. She would have to be respectful of his feelings, even though she was not at that same point. She would keep her own warming up feelings to herself. Thomas was a good friend and she certainly didn't want to hurt his feelings. How would she feel if this were her own son, Luke? She would want him to be happy with a family of his own. She wasn't sure that she wanted the fine women back home waiting for him."

Liz looked back at the beautiful quilt and tucked the letter in the Bible on the table.

"I didn't mean to read it," she thought. "It just fell open in my hand."

She surveyed the room and it looked almost cozy. It would need a rug on the floor and some fresh curtains as soon as she could get to them.

Sounds were now coming from below and she started to the stairway as Megan appeared.

"Liz? Oh my, where did that quilt come from? Does it belong to Thomas?"

Megan was as drawn to it as Liz was when she pulled it from the box. She started to inspect the pattern and workmanship.

"Who made this? I don't recognize the work. It is very good."

"Thomas' mother made it and gave it to him as a gift. It is lovely, isn't it?" Liz answered her sister.

"Well, it is really pretty. I don't think that I have seen a log cabin like that before. The red triangles," Megan paused. "I like them but they almost look like they are keeping something out."

Megan looked about the room and said, "It looks nice up here. The furniture will work well. Not quite homey as it should be. What do you suggest, Liz?"

Megan sized up the room and the quilt quickly. She continued to look around the room, taking it all in.

"I think some new curtains; maybe a red check and a rug would fix it up real fine."

Liz looked the room over again and tried to see Thomas living there.

Megan stood and went to the window to see what the view would be.

"His view is good of our house. The large trees in the back are really in a perfect spot. We can get someone to build us a porch on the back and the house will work well. We must sleep two to a room but they are a nice size. And the kitchen is convenient. We have a large wood-burning stove. Samuel… um, Mr. Smith is seeing to the wood that we need to get started."

Liz moved to the window where her sister was standing.

"Well, it sounds like we lucked out. It even came with a garden. I'm really surprised over that. But it looks like it needs to be tended. The rain has put the weeds into full growth and some vegetables need to be picked. It seems that the lady of the home has been gone several weeks."

Liz could see the weeds from the upstairs window as they peered out. She ignored Megan's slip of the tongue on calling Mr. Smith by his first name.

"I'm finished here, and ready to see how the doors are coming along on the store front."

The two sisters went down the staircase, along the back of the mercantile storeroom and through the storefront where Thomas and Jackson worked on enlarging the front entrance. Both men had smiles of admiration on their faces as they watched the women approach.

"Miss Megan, how is it coming along at the new house?" Jackson asked.

"Just fine, but we need an easier way to get water. The river is so far away. Can we get a well or a pump?"

Jackson was puzzled that they had not found the pump in the back.

"Did you go to the building in the back? They had a pump put in and made a bathhouse there. It is quite fancy. The wife was always ready to go back East and the captain was always doing something to get her to stay a little longer. I think you women will enjoy the luxury of the tub. Many would be willing to rent it from time to time if you got a notion to run a bathhouse."

Jackson had given some most welcome information and they were eager for the time to come when they could use the fancy bathhouse. Megan picked up her skirt and moved quickly toward the house.

Liz lingered a moment longer by Thomas, looking at the new entrance.

"The doorway is looking good. Do we have any red paint? It would be perfect with some on it."

Thomas chuckled at her. "You would like red just about anywhere."

She looked humorously at Thomas and lengthened her step to catch her sibling. She almost forgot, and then turned to say, "The upstairs is all ready for you. I will bring you a rug in a few days when I finish it."

Jackson said. "I do know where some red paint is stored. Let's finish these doors and get ready to go to Miss Anna's supper. She is a real good cook."

As the two women came upon the little building that Jackson called a bathhouse, they found an outdoor pump to a well and a large flower garden. They admired the flowers in full bloom and picked a few to bring into the house, minus a few ants that Liz shook off. Megan turned the wooden latch on the door and pushed it open, not sure what she would find inside. Both women dropped their mouth open when they saw a large footed tub in one corner with drying racks for towels. Then they spied a simple heating system that would allow for plenty of hot water for bathing. It looked like a cook stove almost, with two open areas for the wood to be placed in and burners above which held two very large containers of water. There was an indoor pump that allowed the water to come right into the heating buckets. Next to the stove was a basket that held an extra supply of wood for heating the water.

Megan went closer to the ornate tub and picked up a glass bottle on a shelf with several other bottles and took the lid off. She placed it under her nose and took a sniff.

"Can you believe all of this? It smells just like lilacs." She took another, deeper sniff.

"I'm certainly surprised. I never expected anything like it. Do you think Abby or Emma has seen this?" Liz asked.

"No, we thought it was a smoke house and we could not see the pump for the flowers."

"Let's keep it to ourselves." Megan teased.

Liz thought for a moment that it would be easier if she didn't have to share with two others.

"It would never work. They would find out and be really mad at us," Liz calmly admitted.

They left the bathhouse and went in the back door to the kitchen. Liz commented that a porch would be perfect on the back. Abby and Emma were just getting ready to start working on the kitchen. They had just completed moving into their bedrooms when Megan informed them, in detail, about the bath tub complete with fragrant salts.

"Well! I have to see this to believe it," Abby commented and walked out the back door with her sister.

Liz took a quick survey of the house and found it all to her liking. It was much smaller than her Riverton home. But, all in all she was more than satisfied with the conditions that they had acquired. It was much better than she had ever thought it would be.

The cousins had just appeared after viewing the bathing conditions and were commenting to each other how glad they were that the captain was so agreeable with the comforts of his wife. It certainly made it more pleasant for them.

"I think the good captain loved his wife a lot and wanted her to be happy," Emma, the youngest, romanced the situation.

"I'm not sure about that," Megan returned. "If you really love someone you would stay with them even in undesirable conditions if necessary."

"It has been a busy day, what do we do next?" Abby asked as she dropped onto a straight back chair by a wooden table large enough to feed eight.

"I think we should get out of these rags we have worn for weeks and put on something we have not seen since we packed in Mississippi!" Emma spoke the truth about their clothing; they were rags.

Abby picked up the edge of her skirt and stated, "The next time I see this skirt it better be at the end of the kitchen mop handle!"

They all laughed and Megan added, "My dress is so thin that my arms have gotten tanned by the sun through the sleeves."

Laughter erupted again and Liz gently tugged at the well-worn waist of her dress as it began to come apart in her very hand.

"I had to keep my apron tied on tight or my dress would have fallen off days ago." Liz held the waist up where the stitches had vanished.

"I can't believe that I had this on when Thomas proposed to me."

Abby and Emma both popped their heads up to see if they had heard her right.

Megan was already looking at her sister to see if she could judge her feelings any better about this new development. She cared about Thomas and her sister and wanted them both to be happy.

Her cousins were excited for her and went to give her a hug and a parade of questions.

Chapter Four
New Friends

nna opened her door and welcomed her guests into her home. It was cozy and looked to have all the comforts of home. She had a clean white apron on over the same dark blue calico that she had met them in. Along the back wall were two doors that opened to a wooded area. She had two tables set end to end with chairs on her back breezeway. Large trees canopied the tables and made a cool spot for eating together. A breeze came through and kept the summer evening enjoyable. Two beautiful scrap patchwork quilts of single squares and thin triangles were used as tablecloths. Crocks with blooming wildflowers were set in the center. Anna had enough chairs set out to include all the people that came on the wagons plus Smithy and Mr. Samuel Smith. Pastor Parker had not made it home yet but was expected any moment.

The women gathered together in the back of Anna's house where she was ready to serve tea in tall metal cups.

Emma approached Anna and said, "I simply can't wait any longer. I have to find out how you control all of your curls. They look so nice and mine are just a wild mess everywhere."

Anna smiled and looked at a lovely young woman with curls that had the best of her in the humid heat.

"Oh, it is bearable with a little beeswax and it is great when the wind blows too. I will show you how to do it and share some of mine with you until we can get you some of your own."

Abby heard Anna and Emma and was excited that Emma had an interest in her vanity and spoke right up to Anna.

Liz was admiring the quilts used as tablecloths and the color pattern that the maker had used, when about that time Pastor Parker rode into a wonderful surprise. The Mailly family had arrived.

Pastor Parker was a tall man with wide shoulders. He had a white shirt tucked into dark trousers that covered his cowboy boots. A black string tie was around his neck and a dark cowboy hat was firmly on his head. He had a nicely groomed mustache with a smile that made you comfortable immediately. He dismounted his horse with his jacket over his arm and a Bible in the other. A leather holster was on his left leg with a colt revolver tucked in it. He looked as if he could have been a gambler or a hired gun until the smile and worn Bible showed up. With wide steps from his long legs he joined the group quickly. He went straight to his wife and bent to give her a kiss and a one-arm hug, as he was eager to meet his guests.

"It doesn't look like Lucas made this trip," Parker said as he looked over the group. "These good folks must be starved for some of your fine cooking. Anna let's sit and pray."

Pastor sat at the head of the table with his wife at his right side. Next to Anna were Liz, Thomas and Luke with John, Blue and Tex. Samuel was at the other end of the table with Smithy, Colt, Chet, Jackson, Megan, Emma and Abby at the end by Pastor Parker.

Parker took Anna's hand and laid his other open for Abby.

"Let's give thanks," his caramel voice began.

Each one followed the Pastor's example and took the hand of the one next to them. Even the Rangers and mill workers at the end of the table followed suit. When Parker spoke it was never a question as to who would follow his command.

"Our faithful God, we worship you and are grateful. Thank you for our safe journeys. Thank you for our new relationships and bless this fine food that my precious wife has prepared."

Parker gave Anna's hand a little squeeze. Liz and the other females all had their heads up watching this powerful godly man. They had never seen or heard a preacher like this one before.

Thomas broke Liz's train of thought when he gave her hand a squeeze at the "wife statement", and she bowed her head.

"And thank you for bringing the Mailly family to us, bless them, oh Lord. And all of God's people said "Amen."

Amen's were heard around the table as each one raised their head.

Thomas continued to hold Liz's hand until he had to start passing the heaping bowls of mashed potatoes and fried chicken.

Megan didn't realize that she had not turned loose of Jackson's hand. She was still into the prayer and voice of the Pastor, and besides, her little hand just swam inside of Jackson's large one. Jackson just looked at Megan and seemed satisfied to let her hand stay there, in his, on his leg. Suddenly she was out of the trance and realized.

"Excuse me, I was just thinking." And she took her hand back to her lap with a little giggle and smile.

Jackson smiled back and thought. "Yeah, me too."

Pastor started the conversation after all the food had gone around the table and praises were given to Anna for all of her hard work preparing the meal. Luke teased his mother that her chickens had barely made it to Texas and that they sure tasted fine. Laughter and good humored teasing were enjoyed all around the table

"Miss Abby," Parker started the conversation. "The families that hired you have appointed men to oversee the school. They are seated at the table with us tonight, Mr. Owen Smith, otherwise known as "Smithy," his son Mr. Samuel Smith and me. They also tell me that they have your wagons unloaded and you are almost settled in."

Parker took a bite of a chicken leg and smiled at his wife with approval. Anna appreciated the way her husband rewarded her with compliments, silent or spoken.

Parker now looked to Liz. "We want to welcome all of you to Fort Worth. If there is anything that we can do for you now or later, please let us know. You can talk to any of us and we will do our best to accommodate you. We want all of you to settle here and plant some deep Texas roots. It is a wonderful place and we are excited that you are here."

Abby looked over the three governing men and was surprised that there were only three, and that Samuel was one of them. Before, at her Mississippi placement she had five and all were older men with families. She didn't know what to think about one being single and a little older than she. But this was the West where everything was different and rules were more relaxed.

Thomas addressed Parker and said. "You said earlier that if you could help in any way to just ask."

"Yes." Pastor acknowledged the request. "What is it, Thomas?"

"This morning I asked Liz to marry me and she said yes. We would like to be married in a few weeks after we get settled. Lucas should be here by then."

Cheers went up around the table and congratulations were handed out to the couple. Thomas smiled at Liz and she smiled back while her stomach was churning in knots. She thought the chicken must be having a fight inside her.

Tex sat back and watched half of the happy couple. Lunch today certainly was no honeymoon.

Megan, as well, was keeping a sharp eye out for her sister and this turn of events. Megan could tell that Liz was not feeling very matrimonial at this point.

After the meal was complete with peach cobbler for dessert, the women went to help with the clean up.

The men stayed gathered around the table discussing a current event. Tex leaned into the table and said to Pastor Parker.

"So, you're saying that a group from here went to Birdville and stole the County records?"

"Yes. As I was riding back from a visit just south of here, I came across old man Jeb who told me that the group had just come back with the records and they want to make Fort Worth the county registrar. Now that the Mailly's are here the citizens think this should be the place for Tarrant county records. It will help to firm up the likelihood that we will be a prosperous town. The county seat brings growth and life to the area and they want it here, at the fort location." Parker was concerned that there might be a fight over it.

Tex leaned back in his seat and looked to Jackson and Colt.

"Guess it's a good thing we are here. We will take a day, ride out at daybreak and look into it. Maybe Birdville won't put up a fuss. We will tell them that the Rangers are aware and that we are handling it. It should stay calm. But if they do we will be prepared. I feel that the records should be here. I'll send word back to the authorities and see what the legal decision is. Where are the records at now?"

Parker raised his shoulders. "I will see if I can find out in the morning."

"Good." Tex said. "See if you can get them to your house for safe keeping until we can get this straightened out and a location chosen."

The other men around the table shook their heads in agreement.

"I think we will call it a night. We are headed to the bunk house."

John and Blue shook hands with Parker and tipped their hats to Miss Anna. "Great meal, ma'am."

When no one was looking, Thomas had slipped away to plan a surprise. He went to the bathhouse and pumped water into the pots to heat and put wood in for the fire. It would be all ready when Liz got home for the night. She had had a long day, and a nice hot bath would be just what she needed. Thomas went back to the group without being noticed.

Anna was asking Liz questions about the wedding and Liz was about to drop she was so tired. Megan scooted a chair under her in the nick of time.

"I think we better get you home." Megan said. "I have your things all unpacked. You can go straight to bed."

Thomas entered the kitchen and said. "I can see you home Liz. I'm sure you are exhausted."

"I'll see you in the morning," Anna said with a smile.

Liz gave Anna a hug and told her thank you for the help today.

Thomas took her hand, as they walked toward the house he said, "I have a surprise for you."

"Oh, Thomas I don't think I can take another one today. It has been full of them," Liz said as she walked toward her new home and real bed.

"Save it for another day," she teased.

"I have been saving them for a long time and now they just won't wait." He grinned.

"Yes, what is it?" Liz managed a smile.

Thomas led her to the bathhouse where he opened the door for her to see inside.

"Liz, the water is hot and ready to pour into the tub. If you want, I can do it and you can go get your nightgown and wrapper. I didn't get the chance to have Megan do it for me." Thomas looked at Liz for her approval.

"Thomas you are too good to me. Thank you so much. This is really sweet. I will enjoy it and yes, pour the water. I'm weak as a kitten."

He kissed her on the forehead and she leaned against his chest. It felt strong under his shirt. Caleb was muscular but not like this.

"Thomas must do more laborious work than Caleb." She thought.

Thomas put both arms around her and said, "I love you Liz. I can't believe that I can finally say that to you. I know that a lot has happened today. You get some rest and we can make plans later, after you have time to warm up to it."

He pulled away from her and smiled to let her know that he had no hard feelings over the previous encounter.

Thomas poured the water into the tub, and then turned to leave. "Goodnight sweetheart."

Liz watched as he walked to the back door of the mercantile and then she went into the house for her nightgown.

Abby was called out to the table where the school board was now meeting.

"We do have a contract for you. You need to read it and then sign it if you agree to the terms. We are very excited to have a fine teacher like you, Miss Wilkes. You came with great marks from your past school in Mississippi. We hope you will stay a very long time." Pastor Parker pushed the papers over to her and nodded his head.

She liked Pastor Parker and was glad that he was the head of the board. She could go to him if the need ever arose. She looked to Smithy and then to Samuel, all seated across from her.

"You will meet all of the families at church on Sunday. We have a picnic planned for our noon meal and then a barn dance with a barbeque, when it cools off…evening time. We would like to have the signed contract before Sunday is over." Samuel spoke with authority to Abby Wilkes.

"I think that will be sufficient time to review the requirements. It also sounds like a wonderful time to meet the children and their families. I will be looking forward to it. Thank you, gentlemen, for the opportunity to teach your children."

Abby looked over at the men and realized that none of them had children who would be in her classroom. Most of them had no children at all.

Megan and Emma were quick to plan a quilting for Sunday afternoon. They thought it seemed like an ideal time. Many women would be gathered for the day. The decision was made to have two quilt frames set up so that all could quilt together. Anna would get word out for their quilt supplies to be brought to church on Sunday. The breezeway at Anna's was the perfect spot to sew and watch children play or take naps at the same time. Two frames set up also allowed Emma and Megan's quilts to be put in the frame to be quilted. It would be a grand day and they could hardly wait.

As the three granddaughters walked home they agreed that with the Parkers in Fort Worth that they already felt like they were home. It had been a good day.

Samuel stood on the porch with Jackson as the women walked toward the old Captain's house.

"It will be good to have them in Fort Worth." Samuel said

"They are a spunky bunch of women." Jackson spoke his thoughts. "And don't try to tell them how to do somthin' and don't get any ideas that they don't agree with. But all in all, I really like the family. I haven't met the grandpa yet. Rumor has it that he is the only one that can tell them what to do and you better not cross him when it comes to his granddaughters. You may not live to speak of it again. He thinks that a war between the states is a sure thing and that is why they moved lock, stock and barrel." Jackson leaned on the porch railing as the women disappeared around the corner to their house.

"Guess they don't need us watchin' to see if they made it home then." Samuel leaned on the rail with Jackson but neither one moved for a long time.

"But, it sure is fun," Jackson thought.

Liz took her worn dress off and folded it on the wooden stool that was by the tub. She looked at it and sighed as she thought about all that it had been through. She stepped into the tub and let the warm water caress her skin. The water smelled like lilacs. Thomas must have sprinkled some of the sweet smelling salts in the water when he filled the tub. She slipped down to her shoulders and wiggled the braid from her hair. She went under the water to soak herself completely. It was wonderful to be in the warm tub of water. She reached for a bottle of thick liquid and poured a small amount into her hand. It bubbled up and she put it in her hair.

"This was a great surprise, Thomas," she thought.

It seemed like she stayed in the water forever. Her fingers started to look like a piece of dried fruit. The fluffy cotton towel was just within her reach and she stepped out of the tub to dry herself with it.

She thought again about the pampering that the captain had bestowed upon his wife. An item like this towel was only found back East in an expensive home or Inn.

Liz put her nightgown on for the first time since she drove the wagon out of the flood. She had decided on that day that a wet nightgown was not what a lady needed to be wearing when driving a team. They would just sleep in their clothing, like it or not. She also decided that was why she had a hard time sleeping as they were going west.

"How could I write this day in my journal?" She thought as she dried her hair in the towel. "It has gone on for an eternity."

Liz pulled the wrapper around her and tied it at the waist. Her damp hair was about her shoulders. She stepped out the bathhouse door and looked about her surroundings. The sounds of the night were humming a slow song and a coyote yodeled in the distance. Liz saw the moon dipped in the sky. It was the same moon she watched from her Riverton home, but it seemed much closer here in Texas. She paused to admire it.

"Thank you God." She silently prayed. "You are good."

Liz took the handle of the backdoor and slipped into the kitchen. She walked to where the two bedrooms were and tried to remember which one she was sharing with her sister. She chose the one on the right and went immediately to turn the quilt down. Her journal fell to the wood floor with a thump. She now knew that she had the correct room and placed her head on her feather pillow, in her new bed.

"I'll write it in the morning," she mumbled as she pulled one of Granny's quilts over her legs. This was one of the few quilts that Granny Claire had ever pieced, for she was an avid appliqué quilter. The long black star points and alternating red and green stars were quite beautiful. Granny had named it Homestead Star. Liz had remembered the story of every new homestead receiving a star quilt for good luck. The women of the community would make it and send it in every wagon going to a new home. It did not surprise her that Megan had chosen this quilt for their bed.

Liz never heard the whispers from the women as they prepared for bed or Tex as he rounded up his Rangers. Luke and the others went to one of the barracks for the night. Even an army bed would be a treat for them tonight.

Chapter Five

The Gift

Mr. Skelly, the peddler, was just about to the edge of Fort Worth when he stopped to take a quick break. He had stopped at a small number of ranches and farms along the way and had traded for a few nice things. He hoped it would be a successful trip. It had been a long time since he had made it this far west. The Comanche that roamed this territory were a mean bunch when they wanted to be, which he thought was all of the time. Since that little nine-year-old girl was kidnapped back in 1836, he had been a little frightened to venture this far. But with the Rangers and the Cavalry roaming Texas, he thought it could be worth the trip to go west. He had heard that the Indians had been pushed out. He still had the letter from Mrs. Sewell tucked away for the Mailly women and the bridal wreath quilt that he had acquired from her also. He saved it back for a special trade.

As he was walking back to his wagon in the morning sun, he saw a man on horseback.

"Hello, anyone there?" Thomas called out as he neared the peddler's wagon.

"Mr. Skelly here." He said in his Irish brogue. "Friend or foe?" the round man asked Thomas.

"Oh, friend for sure Mr...."

"Skelly, just peddler Skelly, and your name?"

"Thomas Bratcher. I'm new to the area."

"Oh," he said, "did you bring your family? Do you need something for them? I have some lovely things. Yes, I do Mr. Bratcher. Would you like to see?"

Thomas smiled over the roundness of the old peddler and his heavy accent. He had to listen carefully to understand what he was saying.

"Yes," Thomas paused, "I brought my family. They are the Mailly's from Louisiana and…"

The peddler's eyes lit up and he made one hop off the ground with a little jig attached to his excitement.

Thomas wasn't sure how the peddler could get all of his weight off the ground like that and had to hide his amusement at the Irishman's actions.

"The Mailly's you say? I have something for them." He talked with excitement as he pulled the letter from his inside vest pocket.

"I have this letter that is to be hand delivered from Captain Sewell's wife back at Fort Polk. Can you show me the way to the ladies?"

"Yes I can. I'm going that way now. But first I might need to buy something from you. Elizabeth Bromont is to be my wife and I need a gift for her. What would you have in your wagon for my future bride?" Thomas asked with anticipation.

The peddler put his finger up as he thought and asked, "Could your bride be the same as a Liz Mailly?"

"Well, yes I think she could. She is the granddaughter of Lucas Mailly and the widow of Caleb Bromont."

"You must get down from your horse, and see what I have for you to buy. It is your lucky day, Thomas Bratcher. Your new bride will love you even more when I show you what I have."

"That's exactly what I'm looking for," Thomas thought and he quickly got off of his horse and followed the peddler to the back of his wagon.

The little man got up in the back rather quickly and proceeded to move things around inside. Finally he appeared with a large cloth bag. He eagerly started to tell him the story of the quilt that was inside.

"Mrs. Sewell, the precious lady, has a new wee one and was in need of many things and she was to buy a special gift for her husband. He is a lucky man to have the love of that woman…yes indeed…well she was to buy a gift for him and to trade for the baby things."

Mr. Skelly was untying the knot at the end of the bag as he told the story and finally was ready to pull the quilt from the bag. Thomas couldn't imagine what it was and why the peddler was so elated with it. But he did say it was the perfect gift for Liz and so he waited to see what it was.

The peddler birthed the quilt from the bag and continued with the story as he opened it wide for Thomas to view.

"She makes all these quilts," the round man continued, "and just has them stacked up and folded so neatly in a cabinet. The women were so inspired by the quilts that they could hardly continue with their trip. Miss Mailly er Liz," the peddler stumbled with what to call her, "really wanted this one and tried to buy it from her that day… to no avail. Mrs. Sewell traded this one to me with strict instructions to only sell it to Liz Mailly. Are you sure your bride is the right lady? I sure would not want to make the Captain's wife upset with me. But if she is…you are a lucky man …yes indeed… the luck of the Irish is upon you today Mr. Bratcher."

The peddler finally stopped talking. Thomas wasn't sure he followed all that the man had said. Thomas just looked at the quilt. It was a circle like a ring, a wedding ring and it had multiple colors of rings. It was beautiful and he knew Liz would love it.

"It is perfect. I will take it and one more thing. Do you have a gold wedding ring?" Thomas asked hoping that his luck was still in full force.

"No, but I do have a sterling silver one that I think you will like as well. It is quite unique in the design," the peddler said as he went to a small box that he had a few pieces of jewelry in.

Thomas was amazed at the inventory that the man had tucked away and hanging in every nook and cranny of this wagon. He folded up the quilt carefully and tucked it neatly in the bag that it came from. He walked to his horse and tied it to the horn of his saddle. Thomas turned around and the peddler had the ring for him to inspect. It wasn't quite what he had in mind but it was very pretty and Thomas thought it was small enough to fit her finger.

"Looks like I owe you some money, Mr. Skelly. How much am I in for?" Thomas was now holding the ring on the end of his little finger.

"Are you trading or have real money?" The peddler was eager to receive cash.

Thomas placed the ring into his vest pocket and pulled out a shiny gold coin.

"Will this be fair?" He asked as the sun blinded the peddler with the reflection.

"More than fair Mr. Bratcher. It has been an honor to do business with you."

"Load up and I will take you into town to meet the women where you can deliver the letter personally. I bet they will even invite you to stay for supper," Thomas told the old Irish man. "And remember…what I bought today is a secret…no telling."

The man, happy as a leprechaun, climbed up into his wagon and placed his finger over his mouth to let Thomas know that he would never tell the women.

It was hard to talk to the peddler as they traveled together into town. The wagon made so much noise from the clanging of everything that dangled from it. It wasn't far though and they were at the edge of the community.

"This way," Thomas said and soon they stopped at the foot of the stairs to the Mailly mercantile.

Liz came to the doorway to see what the noise was with a dust cloth in her hand and a thick braid down her back. She had a different calico dress on today. It was an earthy brown with small flowers across the cloth and some random dots. The apron was different also. It was a dark tan check with little flower branches scattered around. Thomas thought she looked rather pretty as she worked on the mercantile.

"Hello, Thomas. Who is your friend?" Liz asked.

"I think he will be your friend any minute," Thomas answered, "and he has a letter for you."

Liz smiled and quickly went to the peddler and asked him to stay for supper. He gave her the letter and said that Samantha and her parents were fine and sent their best regards. Megan and her cousins came from somewhere and looked over Liz's shoulder as she opened the letter. As she finished reading it, Megan took it and moved it closer so the Wilkes could see the contents better.

"Thank you, Mr. Skelly. It is an unexpected pleasure to have a letter from friends. Will you be going back that way?" Liz asked. "We will write one for you to send back whenever you pass her way.

"Sooner or later I always make it back to Fort Polk. I will be happy to take her one." The peddler pulled his watch from the tight pocket at his girth.

"Take it easy for a while and we will find you for supper. Emma will finish up soon with it. Do you pass our way often?" Liz quizzed the peddler.

Thomas thought that Liz had as many questions as the peddler did.

"No, not really. But if the place becomes stable, I will return." He paused and looked at her storefront. "Looks like you could use some glass windows for your new business."

"Yes, I need to have some sent our way when Thomas returns with the first load of freight." Liz looked at the doors that required windows and the front of the store that desired them also.

"If you like small window panes, I have them on my wagon now. I think that I have enough to do what you need." The peddler turned to retrieve the windows from the back of his traveling store.

Liz tucked her towel into the waist of her apron and quickly stepped down the stairs to the wagon. She stood with Thomas to see what Mr. Skelly had.

"This man has everything in his wagon," Thomas thought as he met at the back of the wagon again. He wanted to see the window panes that he would be putting in the front of Liz's mercantile. After careful inspection Liz was more than satisfied.

"Yes, we will take them all." Liz looked to Thomas for approval. "What do I owe you Mr. Skelly?" Liz asked, and retreated for her payment in coins.

Chapter Six
Church on Sunday

The sun came up that Sunday like it was Easter morning. It just looked like it had a message to give the world of hope and peace. The rays shot down comfort and happiness to all who would receive it. Liz and the others had slept in the day before as well and they felt well rested on this glorious Sunday.

Liz was adjusting to one of her new garments as well as to a new relationship with Thomas and her stomach felt better this morning. It was a good choice to marry Thomas. He was her friend as well as a good man who loved her. She would settle in to her new position as Thomas' wife.

Megan was right about it being a good decision; it was growing on her. Thomas was just so excited that he could be out in the open with his love for Liz. She needed to become accustomed to it. He was humorous to watch.

The dresses came out that had been packed away for months and the women were anxious to get fancied up for the church meeting and the day of festivities. Finally it was time, and they walked out the door to go to the church.

It wasn't a very long walk to the church or to Anna Parker's house. They chatted with anticipation as they walked part of the way on the wood sidewalk and then across the dirt street to the other side. They stepped along a trail made by others before them who also were going to the church or the Pastor's home.

Abby thought about the school children that would soon be treading the same path to her classroom. She would be meeting the families today and she wanted to make a good impression. She looked down at her attire and smoothed a wrinkle that did not exist.

"Do you think we dressed up too much?" Abby asked no one in particular.

"Well," Liz paused, thinking it over, "most will just have on their best cotton dress and newest bonnet." Liz looked the group over and they did look a little out of place for frontier life. "We do have nice bonnets on," she added.

Megan had a concerned look on her face. She had not thought this one out and she was a little worried about making the others feel uncomfortable. She did not want to be unapproachable by the other women. She had been looking forward to meeting them and making friends.

"We must not appear uppity," Megan spoke, "but I do want them to see what lovely dresses I can make for them or teach them how to make on their own. Let's go back and take our layers of petticoats off so that our dresses will appear less fancy. Remember the good book said to wear our best to worship the King and we will." Megan felt satisfied with the suggestion to the others.

They had decided to turn around when Anna saw them and called out a greeting.

"Good morning, don't you all look lovely." Anna praised the women and reassured them. "Come and meet some of the others."

"We were about to turn around." Liz said to Anna who was now next to them.

"Why? Is something wrong?" Anna asked the group of well-dressed women.

"We are afraid that we are over dressed and we do want to make the proper first impression with the town's people and Abby's students," Liz informed Anna.

"You look very nice, and I think they are expecting you to be a little more cultured. I do believe that is what they are looking for. Word has spread quickly that you are here and that all of you are exactly what we ordered for Fort Worth." Anna soothed their worries and took Liz by the hand moving them in the direction of the church. "Most everyone has arrived and they are visiting by the shady side of the church."

As Anna gathered the women closer to the church building, voices and laughter could be heard. Two children ran from around the corner and stopped in their tracks as they saw the ladies coming toward them. The youngest of them spoke out loud and said, "Look Sissy...they's so pretty. Just like Ma's weddin' pitcher."

The oldest put her arm on her sister's shoulder to bring her close and smiled at the beautiful women who were now before her.

Anna spoke first and bent down to the girls' level. "I want you to meet my new friends and your new school teacher." Anna motioned to each one as she introduced everyone. "And this is Abby Wilkes, your new teacher."

Abby reached out to take their little hands. "Lillie, Daisy it is so nice to meet you. I can't wait to have you in my classroom. Do you know how to read?"

"A little, Miss Wilkes," the oldest one spoke proudly. "Mama went to school back East before she married Pa and she done teach us some. I can get some of the words in the primer and Sissy knows all her letters."

The youngest one was excited to talk to her new and pretty teacher. She started to recite her numbers for Abby.

"That is very good. Let's go and meet the others." Anna moved them to the shade where the crowd had gathered.

"Good morning church family." Anna called out in her sweet voice to get their attention. "You have met the men this morning that have traveled from Louisiana and now I would like for you to welcome warmly the women."

Before Anna could get all four names out, small groups gathered around each one with smiles and handshakes. The church bells rang out and the citizens of Fort Worth went up the steps to hear the word that Pastor Parker would preach.

Liz and her family sat on the left side of the church a few rows from the front. Behind her were the others that had traveled with her. Thomas sat closest to her right with Anna at the aisle. A few of the ladies went to the front to sing and two men with musical instruments played also. Liz did not know the men and could not recall the names of the women, but they played very well. She enjoyed the warm lively sound of the harmonica played by youngest man. "When the saints are called up yonder" never sounded so good.

Her attention was diverted to the pew benches on the other side. A large white dog was standing and singing the tune right along with them and seemed to know the song quite well. Liz glanced around to see if the singing dog amused anyone else. No one seemed to notice. Pastor prayed and the dog bowed his head. Parker welcomed the guests and the dog looked around to see who they were. Liz was sure that the dog winked at her when Parker welcomed her. Parker asked the congregation to be seated and the white furry member took his pew also.

Liz smiled and lifted her hand to cover her mouth. She thought that she would start laughing out loud. She could feel it bubbling up inside of her and she twisted in her seat, hoping to detour it. Thomas looked down at her and she pressed her lips together. She didn't want to look at Megan. She knew that if their eyes met and she was watching the dog too that the laughter was sure to come out. The more she watched the dog participate in the worship service the more her shoulders shook.

The group was now settled in for the message and the dog sat in the bench attentively. No one else seemed to be paying any attention to the furry church member. Megan finally reached across Luke and grabbed Liz's hand firmly. The two sisters would not look at each other but the church pew shook with repressed laughter from the two several times during Pastor Parker's sermon. The dog even barked an appropriate amen a time or two that almost broke Liz and Megan into an outburst. Liz hoped that she would not have to carry on too much of a conversation after church about the lesson. She had not heard a word that Pastor had said.

Finally the service was over and Liz turned to Megan to let the tension release. They laughed and gave accounts of what they thought they saw the dog do. Anna joined in the conversation with a giggle of her own and explained.

"Angel belongs to Parker. He has always practiced his sermons on her. Everyone here knows Angel. I'm sorry we didn't tell you about her," Anna apologized. Anna continued to laugh a little watching Liz and Megan who were not completely finished with their laughter.

Megan held her stomach. "I have never behaved like this in church before."

"It just struck me so funny," she laughed again, "the dog knew just what to do." Liz held her Bible in her hand and reached inside the cover for a hanky. The joking had brought tears to her eyes.

Suddenly a scream was heard from outside and the women in the church building quickly followed Anna out the back side door. Children were playing on the shady side with adults scattered about visiting. The trio saw a small girl playing with a baby doll next to a fallen tree trunk. A large prairie rattler had been disturbed and was angrily shaking his fat tail at the little girl. She was frozen to her play area and could only let the one scream out. The snake was very close to her and would not have to leap far to have his fangs in her upper torso, which would be certain death for the small child.

Liz and Megan both sized up the situation mentally and knew that Liz

49

had a better aim than Megan at that range. Mrs. Bromont retrieved her small pistol from her church handbag and blew the head of the snake off. The snake's scaly body fell over the small leg of the child and she screamed for the entire state of Texas to hear.

Her mother had now reached her and had her gathered into her arms of safety and reassurance. The little girl wept against her mother's shoulder. She looked toward Liz in silence with huge tears gliding down her face.

Megan looked about and saw the congregation standing in silence as they witnessed the saga. The scream and gunshot had their attention.

The father of the child walked up to Liz and put his hand on her gun to lower it. He took her by the shoulders to look down into her face.

"Mrs. Bromont, thank you. You saved the life of our child."

Liz shook herself out of the moment and answered. "Is your daughter hurt?"

"She is fine, thanks to your quick thinking and good aim."

Tex was close enough to see the whole thing and was amazed at what he saw. These dainty, city looking ladies could hold their own in most any environment. He took his hat and brushed it against his leg in pleasure, muttered something and then placed it on his head. He watched the crowd tell each other what they saw or heard and the women were instantly respected by all at this point, even in their fancy city clothing. Liz had saved the life of the small child.

Samuel, Parker, Thomas and Jackson had been enjoying a good conversation when the cry rang out. They were close enough to see the story unfold and watched as Liz took aim on the head of the serpent.

"Did you know that she was that good of a shot?" Samuel asked Thomas.

"I knew she had a gun and that she could shoot...but she always amazes me with her hidden talents," Thomas answered.

"I'm impressed." Parker patted Thomas on the back.

"I'm surprised that Megan didn't shoot the snake," Jackson said as Megan came up beside him.

"I would have, but we all know that Liz can shoot the eye of a sparrow at most any range." She smiled and stood next to Jackson.

Parker called out, "Let us give praise to our God, for He is good. Let's get these tables set up so the women can get our lunch baskets put on them."

When the eating was over and all the children had settled down in safe places for a nap, the women became anxious to get the two quilt frames set up. Anna's backyard was a perfect spot with a cool breeze blowing on that Sunday afternoon. The frames had two beautiful quilts in them.

"Emma, you must name your quilt. What will you call it? It is a nine patch something," Anna said as she threaded her needle to start on the red squares.

Emma stood back for a moment, admiring the top stretched in the frame. It was pretty with those triangle corners. The setting gave it a two-block interaction. "Maybe, Emma's Folly!"

"I like it." Megan said. "And I will call mine, Megan's Feathered Star." It had twelve beautifully pieced feathered stars. Each center was a different star block with intricately pieced triangles. Black star points with red feathered points continuously flowed through the quilt top.

There was a nice turnout of women to work on the two quilts in the frames and the afternoon went quickly. Liz concentrated on learning all of the names and who belonged to which family. She thought that was important and would help Abby with the school children as well.

Three young women were pregnant with their first child and a lot of the talk was about babies. Emma picked up her thimble and scissors and moved over to the feathered star quilt. "Megan, do you have room for me at your frame? I do want to quilt some on your pretty star."

"Sure. I will trade spots with you so I can quilt some on yours. It is almost complete, I better hurry."

As they passed each other, Megan leaned over to whisper in Emma's ear. "Too much baby birthin'?"

"How did you know?" Emma asked with a smile.

The day was growing long and new relationships were being formed. Parker and Liz both went to get a drink of water at the pump where a table had been set up for the drink station.

"Having a good time?" Pastor Parker asked the new town hero.

"I really am. I didn't know what to expect. I feel like this is home already." Liz took a drink. "Yes, I really like it here."

"I talked with Thomas some today, about the wedding, and Caleb. If you need to talk about it, or anything, Anna and I are always here for you. And remember that it stays with us. We care about you and all of our flock. If it helps, Thomas is a good man and I have never seen anyone as smitten as he is with you."

Liz listened to what her new friend and Pastor had to say. She decided to confide in him. It seemed that he could look straight through her anyway.

"Yes, I know that about Thomas, and I do care for him. He has had a long time to think about this and it is new to me. He is ready to jump ahead...and...I still feel married to the one I loved. I don't know if he can give me the time I need," she paused, "to learn to depend on him."

"You will. Time will help." Parker switched topics. "By the way, good shooting today. That family has already lost one child. Another death would have devastated them." Pastor Parker smiled at Liz and walked toward the men at the fire pit where a large animal was roasting.

The afternoon was turning to evening and Abby decided to look for the school board members and give them her decision.

Samuel and Parker looked over the contract that Abby Wilkes presented to them with a perfect penmanship signature at the bottom. They were really pleased with their schoolmarm, Abigail Victoria Wilkes.

"When would you like school to start?" she asked.

The two looked at each other and then back to Abby.

"What do you think?" Parker asked them both. "We could start with the younger ones and then add the older boys after harvest."

"That sounds good. We can pick a date in a few days," Abby said to the board members as she shook both of their hands to seal the deal.

"I have an announcement to make and then we can get ready to eat again," Pastor called out and laughter came back to him.

The citizens gathered around again and listened to what would be said. The lives of Tarrant County were changing today.

Pastor cleared his voice so he could be heard well. "We are waiting on final word for the permanent location of the county records. We have reason to believe that the location will be here." Cheers went up from the crowd. "We also have a signed contract for our teaching position. Miss Abigail Wilkes has accepted the assignment with a signed one-year contract."

Hoops and hollers were let out by the parents and children alike.

Pastor held his hands in the air to calm the crowd and they quieted down. "We will announce the first day of school soon. Let us know what suits you. We plan to let the harvest hands start at a later date."

This time the older boys sent out a cheer of excitement.

"May I introduce to you our new teacher, Miss Abigail Wilkes?"

Abby felt the color come to her cheeks as Parker made the announcement. She felt so special, welcomed and privileged to be teaching this group of students. They really wanted to learn. She approached the front where the pastor spoke and faced the crowd. The sun was starting its descent in the west and a warm yellow glow surrounded the town. Abby looked out over the crowd and saw her sister and cousins with big loving smiles clapping and cheering for her. The little town in Mississippi never cheered for her. Her heart beat fast inside her yellow dress. As her eyes scanned the crowd they stopped when they saw Samuel. He was clapping and he winked at her. She quickly looked to pastor Parker for security.

"I want to thank you for the opportunity to give knowledge to your children. I do take this privilege seriously and I hope you will also be encouraging them to keep up with their assignments."

Abby began to walk away as Pastor stopped her. "One more thing," he paused, "Mrs. Longmont and the others would like to present you with a welcome gift."

Katie Longmont came to the front with a large fabric bundle. With the help of another lady they opened a beautiful schoolhouse block quilt.

"We want to welcome you and give you this quilt in appreciation." Katie spoke softly but with confidence. "Each family made a block for each child that you will teach. We quilted each of those names into the block. I would like for each student to step forward when I read your name."

The last three she called were her own children, "Daisy, Lillie and Daniel Longmont. Daniel will start next year but he really wanted to have a block in the quilt." Katie smiled as her children acknowledged the new teacher.

Daisy spoke out. "The setting stars in the quilt are for good luck and good marks on our assignments." She smiled shyly and twisted at the waist.

Abby was overwhelmed as she looked into the faces of her pupils. This was the best decision she had ever made, to teach in the frontier where learning was such a gift.

"Thank you so very much." Abby beamed." I will treasure it always."

"Well, this certainly is the night for surprises." Thomas turned Liz to the east. "Look who is riding in as we speak."

Chapter Seven

Lucas Mailly

A chestnut mare was stirring up a lot of dust as it galloped closer to the festivities on the church grounds. The aged rider turned the horse to the congregation and pulled back on the reins to slow down. Even in the dusky darkness Elizabeth could tell that it was her grandfather and moved quickly toward him. The other three granddaughters picked up their skirts and ran to meet Lucas Mailly.

Lucas could see that a party was going on and it didn't take him long to see that it was for his girls. He could feel that they had been well received and that his plans were going smoothly. His granddaughters were anxious to see him and were coming to him with smiles. They looked well and they had made it safely to Fort Worth, Texas.

Liz was the first to reach him and she threw her arms around his neck. "I did not expect you so soon."

"You didn't think that I would let you have all the fun did you?" Lucas gave her a firm hug and turned to the others who had now reached him.

"You look well." Megan hugged him.

"As do you," Lucas kissed her cheek.

"We thought you would be much later," Abby said as he put a large arm around her and Emma and pulled them to their toes in a big bear hug.

"Sir, it is good to see you so soon." Thomas shook hands with the man. "Looks like the trip went well for you. Are you alone?"

"Yes, I traveled alone and made better time that way. The timber contracts went quickly and I just couldn't stand to be without my girls knowing that they were having all the fun."

Thomas slapped him on the back and laughed. It was good to have a family he thought. "Let's go over and meet the folks of Fort Worth."

Lucas Mailly and his kin walked closer to the group that had been watching the reunion. They saw a family unit that was knitted together in love and respect. This was the gentle giant of a man who had big ideas and was not afraid to live them and share them with the people he loved or cared about. This man would not allow the women in his life to be weak or dependent. He gave them strength, courage and the desire to take life by the reins and direct it where they wanted.

Liz was already stronger just by him being there. She could feel it in her bones. She was not aware that he did that for her until now. She had never been apart from her grandfather before. She was able to make the trip without him because he expected her to and believed that she could do it. She looked up at him as they walked to the group and placed her arm around him for another hug. He looked down at her as one tear crept out of the far corner of her eye. He reached over with his rough lumberjack thumb and gently took the tear from her.

"I'm here now Liz, none of that."

Thomas saw the interaction between the two and realized for the first time that Lucas would always hold the number one place in Liz's heart. If her grandfather wanted her to do it, she would bite the bullet to accomplish the task.

Luke stopped his fun with the group of boys he had been playing catch with and saw that the commotion was his great grandpa. He had come out of the blue and was now before him in Texas. He ran to meet his namesake.

Liz thought for a moment that Luke might knock him down. Lucas messed his hair up and gave him a good-natured shove at the shoulder.

"You should have seen Mom today. She blew the head of a snake right off before it could strike."

"You must be the famous Lucas Mailly." Pastor Parker greeted him with an out stretched hand. "It is good to finally meet the man that raised the fastest gun in Fort Worth."

"Tell me about this. It sounds like I missed a good story," Lucas said.

The men were all gathered to make acquaintances with Mr. Mailly and the story of the snake was told. Lucas smiled as he heard how the life of the child had been saved.

"It does not surprise me much." Lucas smiled. "Where can a man get something to eat around here? It sure smells better than what I have had on the trail."

The barbeque turned into full swing with an abundance of music and good food. The tables were spread with dishes of food brought by all of the towns' people to welcome the new Mailly family. Lucas had arrived just in time to join in on the fun. The same man from this morning played the harmonica in an upbeat tune along with several other men with fiddles, guitars and drums. You couldn't help but tap your toe and look for a companion to join you in the dance. Some were filling their plates as others took the hand of their partner and hurried on to the make-shift dance floor.

All of the granddaughters of Lucas Mailly had more dance partners than they could circle the floor with. Megan loved the adventure of meeting all of the single men and swirling around the floor with them. An older man, twice her age, kept coming back for a dance. Finally Megan took a break and went to the punch bowl for a glass of cool refreshment. Liz was there and quizzed her on the older gentleman.

"Megan, why are you dancing with the old man?"

"Well," she tried to catch her breath and take a drink, "he is a really good dancer and I can let my guard down with him," she giggled.

Liz shook her head at her impish sister and noticed Thomas coming her way after a conversation with Lucas. Megan was approached by another cowboy and was wheeled off to partner with him as the Virginia reel was starting.

Thomas bent down close to her ear and said. "Let's step away from the music."

He placed his hand on her elbow and steered her over to the steps of the church where they could hear each other better.

"Are you having a nice time?" Liz asked still tapping her boot to the song and looking over to the dancing. "This has been a wonderful day, meeting everyone and Lucas arriving. I was so surprised and relieved that he was safe." Her head bobbed with the music that danced on the night air.

Thomas wanted all of her attention and kissed her. She looked up to Thomas and smiled.

"I'm sorry, you wanted to tell me something and I'm just going on."

"Yes, I talked with Lucas and told him of our plans to marry." Thomas looked her in the eyes the whole time he was talking while resting one arm behind her on the porch railing. "He gave us his blessing."

"Did you expect him to say no?" Liz inquired. "I even think he planned the trip for you to go and him to stay so we would choose to be together."

Thomas thought that one over. "Well, maybe he did. It worked."

"And so it did." Liz stated.

They listened to the music and laughter for a few minutes. Liz really enjoyed the instruments and the liveliness it provoked. Thomas reached under the stairs and pulled out the fabric bag he had purchased from the peddler.

"I have a gift for you." Thomas said.

Liz took the large bundle and untied the end wondering what he was up to now. She pulled out the circling wreath quilt that Mrs. Sewell had made. Her mouth could not form the words she wanted to come out. "How did he get this?" she thought.

Thomas decided to help her out and he said. "I bought this from the peddler. He told me that you had wanted it when you saw it at Fort Polk."

She was speechless as she ran her hand over the tiny quilting stitches and then she placed her hand on Thomas' cheek.

"How did this happen?" Liz asked excitedly.

Thomas was delighted that she was overjoyed. The peddler was right in the fact that she had really wanted it.

"Mr. Skelly told me that you had liked it when you were at the fort with Mrs. Sewell. She only sold it to him after he told her that he was coming this way and he was to find you with the letter too. It was just luck that I was able to get it from him and surprise you with it."

"Thomas, you treat me so well! You can't keep this up."

Thomas was encouraged that this was going well, even better than he expected. "Liz, will you accept this bridal wreath quilt as your engagement gift?"

"Oh, Thomas! It is beautiful and perfect. But I don't have a gift for you."

"You don't need one if you will say yes and marry me right away. With Lucas here we have no need to wait."

Liz was taken aback that he was ready right now.

Thomas repeated. "So Liz, I would like to be married right away since Lucas is here now. Why wait?"

Liz looked at Thomas, the echo of why wait bouncing on the walls of her heart.

"I...I just thought I would have a little time is all. Thomas you are so sweet to me, and the quilt is so exceptional. I don't want to hurt you. I just need some time is all. I'm sorry. You planned this to be special and now I have ruined it and hurt you. I'm sorry." She turned to hide her tears.

Thomas didn't know what to do. What was this strange creature saying to him? He was not ready to give up but she pushed away just as he thought they were making progress. He had made her cry just by loving her. He felt confused and turned to step away. If he was pushing her, then he would step back. Thomas placed his hands on her shoulders. Her back was to him and he leaned into her hair and whispered.

"Liz, I love you and I want to marry you right away. I see no reason to wait. We don't need to court; you have known me longer than Caleb. You know the man that I am. I told you that I could live with the memory of Caleb. All you have to do is try to love me half as much. We have the blessing of your family. We all spoil you because we love you and you are an incredible woman. You have to decide if you want me. I have already waited my whole life for you and I will only wait a little longer. In the morning at dawn put the engagement quilt in the chair at the back door where I can see it and we will set a date to be married. If I don't see the quilt, you will get your wish. I love you Liz; make a choice." Thomas kissed her hair where it was warm from his words. He turned and walked away.

Liz turned to where Thomas had stood and looked for him. She saw Parker speak to him and then he looked her way. Parker placed his hand on Thomas' shoulder, which still stood strong. Thomas never looked back again.

The music wasn't imploring anymore and Liz was not in a party mood. She was upset that Thomas had stood his ground with her and she was mad because he was right. Not many had the guts to tell her she was wrong; Caleb never did.

Thomas sat in the rocker by the upstairs window above the mercantile. He had a perfect view of the house where the Mailly women lived. He watched as Liz came home only moments after he had. Next was Abby and Emma; they chatted as they went inside. Megan walked home with a tall cowboy who had kept her on the dance floor most of the night. She thanked him for walking her home and turned to go inside. He took her by the arm and said something. Her face was frowned and she tried to wiggle free from his grip.

Thomas decided that was enough and took the steps down to the door three at a time. He surprised the young man as he bolted from the door and across the yard. The young man turned loose of Megan.

"Time for you to go home cowboy and tell your friends to stay home with you." Thomas firmly stated to his face.

"I didn't mean any harm," the cowboy said, "just making the lady feel welcome is all." He tipped his hat to Megan. "Thanks for the dancin' ma'am." He backed away and turned to walk across the yard.

"Megan, don't be a flirt. The men will get the wrong idea." Thomas was short and stated it more firmly than Megan had ever heard from him before.

"Thank you, but I can handle it," Megan bristled back.

"Megan you don't weigh more than his leg. You are going to get caught in some trouble. Why didn't you walk home with Jackson or the others?" Thomas returned more calmly.

"I was," Megan said, still a little upset with Thomas, "but they left without me and Tex took Jackson and Colt back to the bunks because they are riding out early. Thomas, what is wrong? I have not ever known you to be angry like this."

Thomas turned to leave but hesitated. "Keep yourself safe and watch out for the others. You're like a sister and I don't want to hear of you getting hurt."

"Thomas, you talk like you won't see me tomorrow. Are you going somewhere?"

61

Thomas took his hat off and held it in both hands twisting it a little. He looked back to where the festivities were coming to an end. "Just be careful Megan and take care of the others." He nodded good night and went to the back door of the mercantile.

Megan watched as he retreated and felt a breeze bringing in a weather system. The temperature was about to change.

Thomas went back to his post watching for the quilt that was to come by dawn. As the sun pushed away the night, Thomas swung his leg over his mare and rode north from Fort Worth.

Chapter Eight
The Truth Hurts

L iz rubbed her eyes as the morning sun peeked in between the gray clouds. The warmth caressed her face. She stretched and pulled the quilt back to swing her legs free and sat up. As she ran her fingers through her loose hair, she saw the circle quilt. Liz bounced out of bed to the window.

"How long had the sun been up?" she thought.

The gloomy morning had tricked her and it was past dawn. Liz gathered the gift from Thomas and quickly walked barefooted and without her wrapper to the back door. She passed Megan in the kitchen who was already dressed and cooking breakfast.

"In a hurry sister?" Megan asked, and flipped the bacon. It sizzled in the cast iron skillet.

"What time is it?" Liz asked as she opened the back door to place the quilt in the appointed location. She shook it by one corner and spread it out big in the chair, easy to see. She stood in her night gown and looked to the back of the mercantile. She saw no sign of Thomas. It was breezy and cool for late summer, and gray clouds loomed overhead. Liz folded her arms across her chest for warmth and modesty. She looked each direction but saw no one. Liz spun around and almost ran to her bedroom to get her clothing on. She must find Thomas.

Megan heard her mutter as she sailed through, almost knocking down Emma in her wake. Emma asked, "What did she say?"

Megan shrugged her shoulders and handed her youngest cousin the fork. "Watch the bacon and I will go see."

Megan entered their room just as Liz was frantically buttoning the bodice of her green calico with red flowers. The dress reminded Megan of a past stagecoach ride when she was just a toddler. She pushed the memory aside and looked at Liz who now was pulling a brush through her hair in hurried strokes.

Liz looked at her sister with concern on her face. "How did I let things get like this?"

Megan did not recall her older confident sister in this mood before. Liz looked at her as she pushed the comb in her hair to quickly contain it. Megan thought she saw tears. Liz was biting her lip and swiped the side of her cheek. "Megan, have you seen Thomas this morning?" the oldest asked hopeful.

"No, what happened?" Megan asked drying her hands on her apron and stepping aside as Liz approached the doorway in urgency.

"If you see him, hold him until I return. I need to find him. I will explain later and don't remove the quilt at the back door." Liz was gone.

Megan went to the back door and saw the bridal veil wreath quilt that Mrs. Sewell had made back at Fort Polk. None of this was making any sense to her. "Emma, she asked,"would you like some buttered bread with your bacon?"

Liz passed the corner of the mercantile and was still on the dirt road. She didn't take the time to get on the wooden walkway in front of the store. She looked both directions but saw little activity in either. She decided to ask at the Pastor's house to see if they had seen Thomas this morning. Lifting the edge of her skirt slightly off the ground she moved surely. Calming herself some and with the scant tear wiped away, she rapped at the door.

"Good morning Anna," Liz quickly said to the Pastor's wife, "I'm sorry to bother you so early, but have you seen Thomas this morning?"

"No, I haven't." Anna sweetly replied. She looked up at the intimidating sky growing thicker. "Do you need help? Parker just went down to Smithy's to get his horse. He is leaving town today to meet up with the Rangers. Looks like rain is in store for us today." She smiled as Liz waved good bye and walked away with quick steps to the livery where Liz hoped to find all the men congregated.

They would surely be there, Thomas included. She had all but forgotten about the county records going missing from the neighboring Birdville community. The wind picked up a little and she wished she had grabbed her shawl on the way out.

As she approached she saw many men but not the one she came looking for. She reached the corrals and Samuel saw her first; he sent a smile her way.

"What brings you out so early in this stormy weather?" he asked as he pulled the strap under the belly of his black mare. Samuel was dressed in his long riding coat. He paused to study her and gave his cowboy hat a tug to secure it better.

Parker had finished saddling his horse. He tucked his Bible into his saddle bag and came to the fence where Liz stood. "Liz, do you need some help?" he asked and buttoned his rain slicker as it flapped in the wind.

Liz looked past him at the men, hoping one more had appeared. The gust had rearranged her hair and the comb fell out and into the corrals. A pony, skittish with the storm, pranced on it and cracked the comb in one step.

"I was hoping to find Thomas with you," Liz stated holding her hair with one hand, trying to keep it from her face as she spoke.

Parker looked at Liz with his news. "Thomas told me last night at the gathering that he may leave early this morning and go north to look at some ranch land. I assumed that you knew."

Samuel had finished securing his bedroll and canteen to his saddle and as he came closer he picked up the broken comb and handed it to Liz.

Sorry," he stated as he laid it in her hand.

"Me too," she sighed.

Samuel spoke next. "Pa said that Thomas was here at sun up to get his pony saddled up and wasn't much on conversation, but he did say that we were not to wait on him to come back."

Samuel's father now joined the group and added his two cents worth. "For what it's worth, I think he planned on being gone for awhile; he had a good size pack with him."

Liz shook her head in understanding. "Thank you. How long will you be gone?"

Samuel spoke up. "We are to meet up with the Rangers south of here. Not sure if there will be trouble bringing the records back, but Tex thought it would be good to have backup and some town authorities present. Parker being a preacher and all will be a calming effect.

Lucas now appeared at the livery with Luke mounted and ready to ride. He was surprised to see his oldest granddaughter standing at the stables. "Liz," he called out, "get out of the weather. We need to ride out this storm. Thomas will be back soon," her grandfather reassured. Her son gave her a smile and prodded his horse in step with the others.

The men of Fort Worth mounted their horses and rode out of the stables. They all touched or tipped their hats as they passed Elizabeth standing in the street. The rain had started and it was cold as it hit her in the face. Samuel looked back as they reached Parker's house. Liz had started to walk home and had reached the mercantile. It boasted new window panes and two new red doors made to order. It looked perfect and was ready to open. Thomas had provided her with everything she had wished for.

Liz went up the steps to the mercantile and pulled open the door. Her hair was slightly wet and the shoulders of her dress were damp. She looked back at the group of riders again, silently hoping to see one more added to the company. She only saw Parker give Anna a goodbye kiss and pray over the band of men for protection. His hardy "amen" traveled on the wind as she stepped inside the building. A gust of wind blew the door ajar behind her and she turned to bolt it. "His room," she thought, "I haven't checked his room." She wasn't ready yet to accept the fact that he was gone.

She moved up the stairs to the living quarters above the mercantile and entered his room. "Thomas, are you here?" she inquired. Only the whistle of the wind disturbing a window answered her. The loft looked much as she had left it several days ago. Some of his clothing was removed from the pegs. "He had packed them," she thought. His Bible was open to Romans 8:12, which read: "All things work together for the good for those who love the Lord and are called for his purpose." A sterling silver wedding band was placed on the open page.

Liz sat back on the bed and placed her face in her hands and cried. She truly was spoiled just like Thomas had said. She played a sad game and had lost. She didn't mean to hurt Thomas or make him leave. She had not meant to keep the quilt inside. She didn't like how things had turned out. She didn't like playing the fool, being wrong or losing control of her life.

"How can this work for the good?" She cried and the storm picked up speed outside the window. The rain came down in steady streams until the street out front was a muddy river. The wind whipped the rain into little needles as it hit the windows and the side of the building. Ting, ting it said as it landed. Thunder boomed and rattled the windows in the red door of the mercantile.

Elizabeth Bromont wrapped herself in the log cabin quilt made by Thomas' mother. She could smell Thomas. She looked to the open Bible from which all of her strength, faith and courage came. She prayed for her family and all of the men on horseback. She asked for wisdom, direction and a second chance, from the God of second chances. Liz wiped her eyes and she heard a prompting in her mind. "My daughter, you don't have control over your life. I do and all things do work together in my plan and my timing." Liz looked around but knew that she would find no one. She had heard that voice before and it comforted her and gave her strength. She smoothed out the quilt, straightened her backbone and confidently went to face the storm.

Chapter Nine
A Still Small Voice

Thomas was inspecting his clothing and bedroll that hung in the tree drying. It had rained for three long days and nights. He spent the next two days rotating his belongings on the branches of a big oak tree. The things weren't dirty, just soaked. He even had to take time off riding so that his horse could dry out as well as his tack. The occurrence had been good for him to think about his future and what he would do. The land was rich and beautiful with small hills, scattered trees and good open pastures for grazing livestock. This was just what he hoped to find. Thomas looked down upon a perfect spot to build a big white ranch house with white corrals full of good horses to breed or sell. Cattle roamed the outstretched hills of the ranch. He envisioned the front of the house and Elizabeth Bromont stood on the porch. He shook his head to make the memory fade, but she was always there. Just like the first time he saw her as a young woman. She had always stood on the outskirts of his life, never really coming in. Thomas poured a cup of coffee from the enamel coffee pot on his campfire. He hoped the coffee would clear his thinking. Thomas kicked the rocks and dirt over his little fire and decided to file on this piece of land and pay the price. The land he wanted was in Denton County close to the Trinity River where it drained into the Elm Fork.

Thomas saddled his horse and packed up his dry things to move on. He was excited about his choice of land and he would keep his plan moving forward with or without Elizabeth Bromont. This place would be close enough to monitor his responsibilities in town. He would most likely place his good friend Chet as foreman on the ranch and Blue would oversee the freight line. Thomas placed his boot in the stirrup and mounted up. He turned his horse to a small settlement called Medlin, Texas.

Thomas rode into the community of settlers; it was just where Tex had told him it would be. He found a small supply store with grain stacked along a table made from barrels. It really wasn't a building, just a roof without walls and a dirt floor. A rooster strutted between the barrels making the hens cluck and move along in the powdery dust of the floor. Thomas stopped his horse and let the reins hang loose as he dismounted. A big man working over a blacksmith's iron next to the supply store looked up, wiping the sweat from his brow with a red bandana. He studied Thomas and stood to greet him.

Thomas took a few steps toward the big man with soot on his face.

"I'm Thomas Bratcher," he stated nodding his head, "I'm looking for Big Moe. I was told I could find him here."

"Who told you that Big Moe would be here?" the man replied in a deep voice as he wiped his hands on the heavy apron he wore.

Thomas stopped and replied, "My friend Tex, a Ranger. He said to talk to Moe about the land that I want to buy." Thomas waited and watched as the blacksmith smiled and all six foot six came toward him.

"I'm Big Moe. Any friend of Tex is a friend of mine." The now friendly giant shook Thomas' hand vigorously, and said, "Which piece of heaven do you have your eye on?"

Thomas couldn't imagine this man not being Big Moe. He blocked the sunlight from view when he stood and the earth quaked a little as he moved. Big Moe's voice was thunderous, he even made the Ranger Jackson look small. Thomas was glad to be able to use Tex as a reference. Moe showed him around the corner to a shady spot with a table. He motioned him to take a seat. Moe still stood and called to a cabin door also nestled into the grove of trees. A young girl, maybe ten came to the opening. She was petite and pretty.

"Yes, Papa," she replied.

"Bring a plate for our friend and a drink from the well too." Moe sat on a tree stump on the other side of the table. He watched as the little girl did his biding. She brought a slice of beef and two slices of dark bread, heavy with fresh churned butter. Thomas didn't realize how hungry he was until he smelled the meal placed before him.

Moe smiled at her and asked, "Is the pie out of the oven?"

"Yes, Papa, it is almost ready. The crust just needs to brown a little more." Her slender body did a small curtsey and she headed back to the opening she had first appeared from. Thomas saw her smile at her Papa with pride as she served the tasty food. He returned the sentiment.

"She has been cookin' for years, every since her Ma passed. As you can see she has her hands full." Moe patted his stomach and gave a nod to Thomas.

Thomas had not had a meal since he left the Sunday welcoming party and he was famished. He had left early, before dawn, just as a storm was moving in. Jerky was all he had in his saddlebag, plus some fruit that he found along the way. Game was hard to find in the rain. He now finished off the last bit of bread and licked some of the butter off of his hand. Moe continued to talk about this small settlement named after Louis and Charles Medlin. About twenty families had come here eight years ago. Moe let Thomas eat without questions. He respected a man's meal time. Thomas had barely swallowed his last bite when the blonde girl appeared with a hot peach pie and a crock of milk. Thomas smiled in amazement as she cut one third of the pie and placed it on his plate. She smiled shyly at him and giggled as she moved the rest of the pie in front of her Papa.

Thomas placed his hands on his tight stomach and laughed as she turned and skipped toward a small puppy that was now headed her way. She sat in the grass and played with the puppy and a rag ball.

"Your daughter is delightful and a good cook," Thomas said over a fork of sweet pie."

Moe looked over to the child and shook his head in agreement with Thomas. "Bethany is good in many ways and I will hate to part with my only daughter. He will have to be a good man or he will deal with me and her five brothers."

Thomas chuckled at the image of a young suitor and the six giant men that would have to approve of the relationship with Bethany.

" She reminds me of her mother, sweet as a honeycomb, floats around happy as a butterfly. It was a sad day when she passed. Do you have a misses and children?"

Thomas thoughts went to Liz. "Well, no, not married," he paused.

"But you have a sweetheart, I can tell," Moe interrupted, "will she not come west with ya? Are ya goin' to send fer her as soon as you get the land?"

Thomas wasn't sure where he stood with Liz at the moment. All he knew was that the quilt was not on the porch. He had waited all night.

"Yes, I do have a sweetheart," Thomas smiled, thinking of her and how excited she was when he gave her the gift.

"Our relationship has taken a bump in the road you might say." Thomas looked at Moe and felt comfortable with the new acquaintance. "I'm not sure that she wants to continue with our plans to marry. She is in Fort Worth, widowed with a half-grown son and very independent."

Moe sat quietly listening to Thomas with his arms folded across his chest. He was leaning back on the stump and an existing tree trunk.

"Is she a good woman?" Moe asked, knowing that she would be.

"Yes." Thomas replied.

"Are you over being mad at her?" Moe intelligently asked.

Thomas snickered as he looked at the wise man.

"How did you know?"

Moe sat up and leaned across the table--it moaned under his pressure. "You said she was independent, means stubborn, you two locked horns, you left mad."

Thomas listened as Moe summed it up so simply.

"Let me tell you how to keep your woman happy." Moe continued seriously. "I was a big clumsy man, no looks, no money. But my Mary she was a looker and could have many to pick from. I just loved her and made her believe in herself, said yes ma'am to almost everything. The sweet thing died birthin' my last son. If you love her, let her know, and give her a second chance. I'm sure she is worried sick over you bein' gone and I'd bet you didn't tell her you were leavin'."

"I suspect you're right. I'll give it some thought."

"Don't wait too long. This life has a way of givin' and takin' and it don't ask us our opinion," Moe looked Thomas in the eye as he gave him the instruction.

"Thanks Moe, for the food and advice. I have some riding miles to think on it." Thomas folded up the paper work for the title to his land and neatly pushed it into his inside vest pocket. He wondered when Moe had managed to get the paper work together. Thomas had gotten more than he planned on, a good meal, advice and an honest friend. That kind of friend wasn't easy to come by.

"We can file your land patent with the Texas Land Office when they send the traveling agent our way if you don't want to travel all the way to Houston," Moe stated, "It's a long way and the agent will be by here in a few weeks."

"Thanks again Moe, but I just feel better taking it there myself. Tell

Bethany it was a great meal," Thomas said, as he let his horse get one more drink at the trough.

Bethany and her puppy ran up to Moe. He scooped the little dog up and snapped him down in his apron bib with one giant hand. The fluffy pup poked his head out of the pocket. The pint size girl was then picked up and a kiss promptly planted on her forehead. Her little arm tried to wrap around her papa's neck, she sat neatly in the crook of his elbow. They both waved and the pup barked as Thomas got up on his horse and began his journey south to the Texas Land Office.

It would take Thomas at least two weeks to make it there and back if he rode hard and had no trouble. Every day he heard the still small voice prompting him to give Liz another chance.

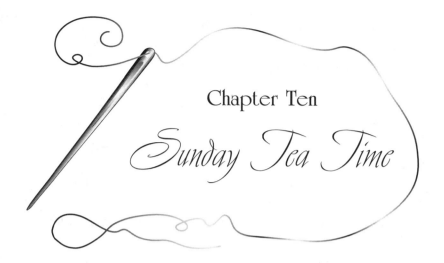

Chapter Ten
Sunday Tea Time

Liz shook the quilt that had taken up a permanent residence on the back porch. She laid it out gently in the chair to reposition it. She was worried that it was getting too much sun and would become faded and weathered. It had now been on the chair for two weeks. Liz smoothed her hand over the circle wreaths and thought of the man that had given it to her.

"How could I have been so stupid?" Liz shook her head in disbelief of the situation. She scanned the dirt road for any sign of his return. All she saw was a dust devil dancing down the road toward the livery.

Megan came to the doorway to retrieve her sister. "Liz don't worry, Thomas will be home soon and all will be well. Come inside and let's get started on our sewing. Anna has arrived. She brought her wonderful molasses cookies. It will be a good afternoon with friends and sewing."

Megan gave her sister a shoulder hug with one arm and went inside to pour the tea into granny Claire's china tea cups. Small red wildflowers with five petals and long thin leafs adorned each cup, saucer and plate. Megan was especially proud to still have the large serving platter now filled with warm, spice brown cookies. The baking aroma took over the room as Liz entered and she went straight to the cookie plate and took two.

Megan was already quilting on her almost finished crackerbox design quilt. The peddler, Skelly had noticed it at supper when he was there and asked to purchase it from her. Megan only had to complete the binding, she was about to finish sewing the first side on the quilt. The carefully cut two and one-half inch strips of fabric were folded in half and pressed neatly. Megan pinned them even with the trimmed edges of the quilt. Her mitered corners were neat and precise. Her needle went in and out the five thick layers of cotton easily. The peddler said that he would return in a few weeks and trade some silks and sateens for the quilt in her small hand. Megan, at ease with her task, started the conversation.

"Anna, I keep forgetting to ask you about the two quilts that you had on the tables, at our first meal together. Did you make them?"

Anna sat stitching on a beautiful blue and cream two tone quilt. It was like a bearpaw block except the triangles for the claws were longer than usual.

"No, my mother did. The blue one is mine. She called it Lickety Split because it went together so quickly, and blue is my favorite color."

Emma noticed how the triangles in both quilts were the same elongated ones. "Look how the shape is the same." Emma stated.

"Yes," Anna said, "Mama had a secret for making all of those triangles so quick and easy. She would put them in almost all of her quilts. She even did it in my brother Samuel's quilt that was on the other table that day. She named it Monkey Tails."

"How did it get that name?" Emma asked thinking back to the quilt that she had seen at Anna's.

"When Samuel was a little boy he saw a monkey on a wagon train that was passing through and was intrigued with the impish creature. So, Mama named the quilt Monkey Tails. He wanted a monkey so terribly bad," Anna smiled and shook her head as she remembered the past.

Emma turned to Anna again and said, "And what do you call this bearpaw quilt?"

"This one has the long claws like the legend down on Bear Creek. Story has it that there is an old bear that lives over at Bear Creek. He has really long claws and he hunts big game just for sport. The bear never eats his prey, just kills for fun."

"Oh," Emma exclaimed and backed away from the blue bear paw quilt. She quickly picked up her new nine patch project, wishing that it didn't have so much black in it.

She had previously decided to call it Emma's Crossroads. As she felt that she was at the crossroads of her life and would soon need to make some decisions about what she wanted. She felt that her life was as boring as the nine patch quilts that she always choose to make. The black represented the somber mood she was in. Emma desperately wanted to break away and find out who she really was.

Liz reached for the teapot to refill her cup and Megan's. "Am I the only one who didn't know that Samuel is Anna's brother?"

Anna smiled at Liz and said. "Yes, Samuel is my older brother and Smithy is our father. Papa has always been the cavalry blacksmith, but he couldn't see going on west with them at this age and we all liked it here, so we all stayed. Parker and I have just followed papa wherever he went, seems like the men needed a minister along with them too. Samuel never joined up. He was just always around after he went back East for his formal education. Samuel is a lawyer but he isn't much for sitting in an office. Said he liked to practice on the open range.

Abby listened carefully to the story Anna told about her family. She was unaware that Samuel was a lawyer. That did explain the detailed contract that she signed and his crafty ways. She looked upon him with a new appreciation, for he was a man that valued education.

Emma asked, "What about your mother?"

"The West is a hard life for anyone; she was a strong good woman, followed papa anywhere--always making a home from nothing. She passed on shortly after we arrived at this post. She was bit by a large copperhead snake in her garden. She is buried at the cemetery here at the church. Mama was quite instrumental in getting this church built and having a real place of final rest, our little cemetery. The only real church graveyard was way over in Grapevine, started in 1851. All of you would have enjoyed her company, I miss her immensely. That is one of the reasons that I'm so glad you came.

Emma took a mental note to be more cautious in the garden.

Megan looked at Liz over the edge of her binding that was coming along nicely. "You have been a bit preoccupied the last few days."

"Yes, I guess that I have." Liz heard horses on the dirt road and went to the window.

"Liz you will never get that multiple triangle quilt started if you jump up every time you hear a wagon or horse on the road," Megan stated.

Abby got up and went to Liz's side at the window. "You poor dear, Thomas will return to you."

Liz took a deep breath and let the curtain fall back in place. "It's my own fault that Thomas is gone. I wouldn't blame him if he never returned."

Liz returned to her seat and started again on the red triangle units. It seemed like she needed a million of them.

Abby felt sorry for her cousin and thought it was best to get her mind on something else if at all possible. "I wish I knew what that quilt was going to look like, Liz. It will be gorgeous I'm sure. The brown and black stars surrounded by all of those red triangle blocks are quite nice."

Megan looked over at the quilt that was barely started. She recalled the original quilt that they had all seen at Fort Polk with Mrs. Sewell. It was an indigo blue. "I thought that you were going to make it blue, like the one we saw." Megan stated.

"I thought about it but then I saw these dark reds and I just couldn't keep my hands off them. These scraps are from one of Granny Claire's scrap collections," Liz admired the fabric as she spoke, "We really don't have too many of her things left."

"Did you get any blocks completed at the mercantile this week?" Anna asked.

"Yes, I do have several blocks completed. I wasn't busy at the mercantile throughout each day, so I did some piecing," Liz replied.

"The mercantile looks nice," Megan stated, "but we do need some more inventory. John, Chet and Blue have been gone for over a week. Grandpa said it wouldn't be any too soon for them to return. They are also organizing more drivers along the way so that they don't have to make the whole trip. In fact, they will be picking up the wagons of freight at the Texas border, close to Marshall."

Emma asked, "Will they bring the rest of the canning supplies? Our garden is bursting at the seams and Mrs. Longmont asked at church today about that."

"I do wish that she could have stayed in town today and stitched with us. She is such pleasant company," Abby said, "She did such lovely work on the schoolhouse quilt. It really is helping me learn the children and their families. It certainly will make the first day of school much easier since I already know their names."

"The canning supplies are on their way as well as many sizes of nails. I've never seen the likes of excitement over nails before. These men think of them like school children do candy. I'm sure the first shipment is spoken for already. It spread through the town this week like wildfire that multiple sized nails were on the way," Liz laughed, "I surely did not get any extra star blocks made on that day."

"What day will school start?" Megan asked.

"I'm just waiting for them to tell me. We decided to let the little ones start right away and the older boys will join us after the crops are in. It will be much easier for the fathers to let them go." Abby had excitement in her voice just thinking of it all. "I also want to start some home visitations. Many of the families have not been into town and I want to invite them personally."

"This week has already gotten busy," Megan started, "looks like Emma and I will be the only ones in the garden and working over that hot stove canning."

Liz was about to finish another set of red triangles. "Abby, will you start the first visits right away?"

"Most likely toward the end of the week, I want to get the classroom prepared first. I would like to start the older girls with some geometry without the young men around." Abby leaned forward for another cookie and brushed a crumb from her lap.

"Will you use a quilt as you did before?" Her younger sister asked. "It went so well when you used your basket sampler quilt. If you need any help, I would be happy to."

"Thank you Emma, I will let you know." Abby placed her sewing in the basket by her chair and let out a sigh. "I have so much to attend to. It would be nice to find someone who would make some donations for the school. There are so many things we need."

"Have you thought about writing back East for some help?" Liz asked.

"Yes, and I must find the time."

Anna finished gathering her piecing into her woven basket. "I will be able to help you with most all of that this week and provide you with a map for the families you need to call on. Maybe Parker can even help you with your travels."

Anna seemed to relieve Abby some with her suggestions and willing heart. She was a good friend to all of the Mailly granddaughters. The gathering of female friends to sew and chat about whatever they wished, without interruption, was a treasured meeting.

"Before I go," Anna looked seriously at the group of women, "I must tell you that I'm greatly concerned over the county records. It is an explosive issue and it is not over yet. Parker and Tex have spoken numerous times on the subject. There has already been gunfire and a fist fight, with one man at Birdville injured badly. Parker has told me to be aware of my surroundings and to be cautious. It could be a while before this is settled and we do hold the records at this time, hidden away. They may try to steal them again."

Liz added to the story with what she knew. "Luke went with the men when they left a few days ago. I had no idea that it was dangerous circumstances. Thomas had left that morning and I was not thinking about trouble other than my own. It was several days before they all returned and Luke said there was a lot of fighting with words, fists and gunfire at times. Tex and Samuel have gone to Austin to try to settle the state of affairs legally. I now understand Samuel's involvement being a lawyer. Jackson and Colt have stayed in the Birdville area to keep an eye on things until Tex returns, hopefully with news that will settle things down. With most of the men away we must be on our toes and stay alert. It is a frightening situation that is bound to be lengthy."

Megan began to make a mental tally of the men that were left in town. Smithy and Lucas were two old men, Luke, an almost grown man, and Pastor Parker. The rest were gone or lived on the edges of town with their families. Farmers and cowboys came and went in town everyday but they would not be aware if the women were in danger.

This new information was concerning to them all and they ended the gathering on a serious note.

Chapter Eleven
A Ride to Remember

Thomas had ridden endlessly to get to the land office. He only had two things on his mind, making the land officially his and Mrs. Bromont. He had thought of a number of ways to approach her, but always found fault with it. What if she had placed the quilt on the porch and he missed it? It was still dark when he rode out of town with the approaching storm behind him. And if she did and now he was away, what would she do? Thomas gave the flanks of his horse a squeeze and urged her on to Fort Worth. He had ridden the pony pretty hard and decided to stop at the next creek to give her a drink and needed rest. It would do him no good to lose his horse as well as Liz. Most likely Liz had lost her stubbornness over the weeks and was anxious to see him as well. His mind flipped back and forth over the issue never coming to a rest. How could one woman confuse him so? This definitely was not as easy as it should be. Heck, if it was always this hard, he hadn't missed a thing by not being married.

Thomas had never been in this part of Texas and it reminded him a lot of his home in Louisiana. He enjoyed riding among the trees heavy with vines and moss dripping from the branches. This was the legendary Sam Houston territory. Houston was instrumental in creating the government of this state which was already rich in history and pride. The settlers were men and women with tremendous spirit and might. Thomas reveled in the satisfaction and gratification that oozed from the pores of the Texans. This unusual state had flown flags under Spain, France, Mexico and at one time was a nation of its own. Since 1845 it had flown an American flag. The brave and loyal people of Texas called it the Lone Star State. Thomas was also proud to be a part of this state and he could now call it home.

As he came over the ridge he saw unexpected riders that he recognized. Tex and Samuel were watering their horses and filling canteens in the shade of a few live oaks. His horse neighed at the sight of the others and their tails swished at the random insect on their back. A slight hint of summer coming to an end was in the air and the nights were beginning to cool down some.

Tex lifted his head as he heard the animals and was surprised to see Thomas in pursuit of the same watering hole. Samuel came around from his horse ready for the coming rider. He moved his hand from his gun belt when he saw that it was Thomas Bratcher.

"What brings you this far south of home?" Samuel asked Thomas. "Looks like you are traveling north to Fort Worth."

"Hello. Yes, I am. I have been to Houston to the land office to file the papers on my land." Thomas patted the vest pocket on his left side. "It will be a great place to raise horses and the likes."

Thomas had now ridden up to the other two. He threw his leg over the back of his horse and proceeded to step down. He shook the hands of his old friends and let his animal drink from the creek with the others.

"Did you have any problems?" Tex, being a lawman, wanted to know.

"No, thanks to you referring me to Big Moe." Thomas slapped Tex on the back and smiled. It was good to be among men he knew. "Big Moe is a mighty big man."

Tex chucked and shook his head in agreement. His horse stamped his front foot in the dirt a few times.

"How are things with you?" Thomas returned the question.

Tex answered, "Good, we are on our way back to Fort Worth. Samuel and I went to Austin to see if we could settle the county record issue. But, I'm afraid to no avail. The authorities told us that it has to be settled among the counties. I'm concerned that there will be a tussle. Someone could get hurt over this issue."

Samuel took one more drink from the canteen and then reached down in the cool stream to refill it. "I can try to defuse it by drawing up a document, but if Birdville won't sign it we will just have to wait it out."

Thomas had completely let it slip his mind. Fort Worth could be in a battle and the Mailly women were in a precarious location. He had assumed that the others were there if the need arose.

"How long do you think?" Thomas asked not caring which one answered. He looked from the old Ranger to the lawyer.

"Could take years to settle," Tex answered and checked the hoof of his painted mare.

"How far are we from home?" Thomas asked again.

"With hard riding, maybe by late afternoon tomorrow," Tex said. He was ready to saddle up.

Thomas filled his canteen, went behind a bush and was up on his horse before Samuel was.

"I have been away for two weeks. Which men are left at the fort?" Thomas asked again as the three began to ride.

"I'm not sure, but I would guess Parker, Lucas, Smithy and Luke," Tex replied, "I think your men went for more freight and Jackson is with Colt, close to Birdville."

Samuel thought, "Two old men, a preacher and a young man wet behind the ears."

"The county seat resides with whoever has the records. Last we knew we did. Parker has them hidden in a safe, public place."

Samuel gave information that could get the women killed. Thomas wondered where that safe place was and who knew about it.

Thomas looked at Tex, "Are you concerned about the welfare of the fort?"

"I could be."

Chapter Twelve

One Fine Day

iz woke early that next morning and went across the yard to the store. She felt revived somewhat and was ready to accomplish some things on her list. Hard work and staying busy were the best way to keep the mind and emotions in order. She would work herself to the bone until Thomas returned.

"Where is Liz off to so early?" Abby asked still dressed in her night clothes and warm from her bed.

Megan went to the back door and stood with her cousin where they both watched Liz marching to the mercantile. "My dear sister will fill every waking moment with a list of tasks that must be completed. That is how she handles her worries."

Abby continued to watch at the door as Megan went to answer the singing teakettle. The steam was waltzing up and making a pleasant aroma as Megan stirred a heaping scoop of sugar into the tea.

"What do you think will happen? You know Thomas well. Will he return?" Abby asked moving her long braid across her perfect posture.

Megan took two tea cups from the cupboard and began to pour the tea. She placed one in front of the chair where Abby was now standing. Abby looked concerned at Megan, hoping for the answer that would restore the situation.

"Yes, I think Thomas will return when he has control of things. He is reserved, but I'm not sure he will continue to allow Liz her way. Caleb never went against her and she is not use to Thomas being a man in charge. I just don't know if Liz will come to terms with the change of power. She is a good woman and strong, but no one is always right." Megan looked at Abby. "I just don't know."

"If he would just return, I'm sure they can work it out. Does grandfather know the situation?" Abby persisted between sips of the sweet tea. She was hoping that he could help and talk to them both.

"Grandpa usually knows about everything. I even think he knows where Thomas is and when he will be back. Notice that he offers no advice or information to Liz. He seems too at ease with things, letting her fret a little with her actions.

Abby was surprised with the words from Megan. But the more she thought about it, the more she thought Megan was right. Grandfather was a cunning man and she loved him even more for his wisdom.

Liz briskly went up the back steps and unlocked the door. She returned the key to her dress pocket. The store apron that she wore was hanging close to the backdoor where she had left it. The door was shut and the frock placed over her head in one swift motion. She stood tying it in the back and then walked to the front where she wanted to rearrange the display of yard goods and sewing notions. First the buttons were poured into a crock and set aside. Then the spools of thread were placed into a wooden box that had held cheese. A note pad was pulled from her pocket to make a reminder to order more thread in tan and trouser brown. The women here were industrious and her thread supply was low. A table to place the supplies on was required and she knew where several barrels were. They had been used by the Cavalry and were left behind. Liz used them to create a long table in the middle of the store. She pushed, pulled and rolled the barrels and soon the long boards were all into shape. A nice display was made, just in time for her new customers of the day. They expected her to be open promptly each morning. Liz stood admiring her work. Tall bolts of fabric lined the floor in between the barrels of the newly made table. Above, flat smaller folds of fabric were attractively displayed on one end of the shelf. Needles and other notions were temptingly arranged and finally, the finished sewing collection was complete. The sun was now above the front window and it was time to open for the day. Liz was satisfied to be a merchant and she took pride in her work. She enjoyed the bookkeeping, ordering the inventory and the conversation with her customers. Keeping the store clean and well groomed was also in her liking. There simply was not enough work at the house with four grown women to attend to the chores. She did like to sew but even that she could not do all day like her sister Megan could. She would enjoy Megan right next door at her millinery and dress shop in the future. Liz stopped for a moment and imagined the hats and dresses next door.

"Maybe even a door between them would be nice. She would ask Thomas about it," she thought, and then she remembered that Thomas was not around to ask and she did not know if he would ever be.

Suddenly, there was a knock at the front door of the mercantile. It was time to open for the day. Liz squared her shoulders and adjusted her thoughts for it to be one fine day. She felt it in the air as she unlocked the red doors and welcomed her first customer for the day. Liz stole a peek down the road, but only saw the sun settling in for another warm Texas day. Liz ran her hand across the top of her damp lip and scolded herself for forgetting her hanky.

"Good morning, I'm Mrs. Perkins. It is a fine day today, you must be Mrs. Bromont." The round, older woman was energetic and friendly. Liz had not met the woman before and was surprised at her lively attitude.

She produced a long list of supplies and Liz started on it immediately. Some of the items were coming on the next wagon and Liz promised to have Luke bring them out for her.

Before Liz knew it, the morning was gone and her stomach began to growl. She had been in such a hurry this morning that she did not even grab a piece of bread. Customers had come and gone all morning keeping her busy filling list after list. She sat for a moment recording the transactions in her ledger and organizing the items to be sent on the next freight wagon. Mr. Wilton wanted a stove for his wife right away. She wondered how his wife had prepared such appetizing dishes at the church gathering without one. Mr. Wilton had assured her that this was her first after ten years of marriage and he wanted to surprise her with the thoughtful gift. Liz thought it would have been more thoughtful if he had done it several years ago. Although, she was grateful for the business and excited that Fanny would have it soon.

Bursting in the back door came her son Luke. "Where are the nails, Maw? We need more nails. Grandpa is putting on those extra rooms." Luke had his hair ruffled a little and the saw dust was sticking to the sweaty areas at his face. He was handsome and looked like his deceased father, Caleb. Liz had not noticed before how much he had grown. Since they had arrived he had been sleeping at the barracks with the men and working with them each day. Liz stood in amazement at the almost man before her.

"Nails, Maw, where did you stock the nails?" he asked again looking at the shelves before him.

Liz went to the correct location and took a box down for him. "How many do you need?" she asked with another box in her hand.

"That's good. Thanks Maw." He took the boxes from her and smiled.

Luke was out the back door in a flash. It didn't even shut between his visits. Liz went to the back door to look at the addition being added to the house they called home. Grandpa was placing a board across a tree stump. He motioned for Luke to hold the end as he began to saw. Liz enjoyed watching her two favorite males working together. Her only son was almost grown, within the year he would be as tall as his father had been. Luke's hair was even lighter now, as the sun had colored it. His face was Texas tanned and his pant legs were growing short over his boots. He certainly did look like his father but, his actions were from his grandpa and Thomas.

"He was turning into a fine man," she thought, "I hope we can get him to complete two more years of school."

Megan was now coming across to the mercantile with a basket. The cloth was neatly tucked inside holding fried chicken, biscuits, garden vegetables and a jar of sweet tea, Megan style. Liz realized that she was famished and stepped out the door to welcome her sister inside.

"Thank you for bringing me some lunch. I left this morning without a thing to eat for either meal. You are a dear!" Liz took the basket from her sister and began to look inside. "Before I eat I need to go out back, can you watch the store for a moment?"

Megan nodded and turned to go out front as Liz quickly went down the back steps to the outhouse. Suddenly, she was in a hurry.

Megan stood in the mercantile admiring the new sewing display when the red door jingled. A dusty bearded man she had not met came in the door and stood, letting his eyes adjust. Megan took the moment to move behind the counter. She felt uncomfortable in his presence, her hand searched under the shelf, for the colt that she was sure Liz had placed there.

"Good afternoon." Megan forced a smile and tried to mentally smooth out her forehead. He was now closer and she could smell the stench drifting from him.

"Surely an outlaw would not smell so bad," she thought and continued to search for the gun with her hand.

"How can I help you?" she asked in a made up cheery tone.

He took his time looking her over and then he looked past her to the back room.

"I need some bullets and some of that sweet stuff there."

She thought he pointed to the peppermint sticks setting on the counter by her hand.

Megan wasn't sure that she wanted to sell him the bullets, but certainly didn't want to make him angry either. He looked at her with a curl on his lips that made Megan think of a snake before it pounces on a mouse. A chill went between her shoulder blades.

"Where is that gun?" Megan thought.

Megan could now see another man standing out on the board sidewalk with his back to the store window.

"How do I handle two outlaws?" Megan thought and was wondering what was taking her sister so long.

"What do you have in the back?" he asked in a ruff tone.

Megan ignored his question and decided to get his bullets. She thought that she could just get him and his buddy gone.

"Help me sweet Jesus!" Megan silently prayed.

The bearded man smiled and his teeth made Megan frown with disgust. The revolting smell increased as he leaned across the counter.

"We could go in the back and have a little fun. My friend will keep anyone from bothering us, it won't take much time. You're a pretty little thing, smell nice too." He breathed in the air like it was Thanksgiving dinner.

Megan turned to take the bullets from the shelf and gagged. She literally thought she would throw up at any moment.

She swallowed the bile taste in her mouth and kept calm. Her quick wit sprang into action. She had the box of ammunition in her hand and clunked it on the counter.

In the most innocent voice that she could find and with her best southern accent she lied. "Why, aren't you a charmer, but I do think my new husband, being a Texas Ranger and all would look badly upon our new friendship. Just a few weeks ago at our church picnic, a cowboy offered me a chair and I thought Jackson would kill him, beat him black and blue before the pastor and all God's people. I surely would hate for that fate to come upon you. I expect him momentarily."

Megan waited a moment for all of it to sink in between the filth that certainly blocked his thinking. He glanced at the door and then back at Megan.

"Jackson that works with Tex is your husband?" he said with a new tone to his voice.

Megan hoped it quivered with fright and respect. She was betting that he knew of the Rangers that rode these parts.

He threw down some coins, not asking for the change, and turned to leave. When he reached the door, he looked back at her. She was positive that under that unruly beard he had snarled at her. The door swung shut and Megan saw him talking to the other man before they left.

Megan's hand went up to her face in a prayerful stance and she sat down on a stool that she instinctly knew was under her. Her forehead was in her hand as she took a deep breath of fresh air.

"Thank you God!" Megan sighed.

Liz came from the back room with two loaded colts. She placed one under the register, where it belonged, and the other under her apron.

"Megan are you well?" Liz stood by her sister and placed her hand on Megan's shoulder. "You did wonderful. I'm sorry the colt was gone, I decided to keep it under my apron and put an extra one under the shelf."

Megan raised her head and weakly smiled at her older sister.

"When did you come in? I didn't hear you."

"I entered when you were in front of the register. I thought it could be dangerous, so I held back. I was about to come and stand by you and slip the gun to you. Thankfully, we didn't have to." Liz started to chuckle as she thought back on Megan's acting. "Do you even know Jackson's last name?"

Megan laughed and released some tension. "No, I don't. I'm glad he wasn't quick witted or we would have been in trouble."

Liz picked up the coins lying by the ledger and flipped them in her hand. "We made a good profit."

"Do we need to tell the others?"

"Maybe. What did he really want?"

"I think he did want the bullets and got an idea when he saw you alone," Liz stated.

Megan lowered her voice to a whisper, "With the gold hiding under the stairs and the county records under attack, we just can't be sure."

Liz shook her head evaluating what her sister said, "I just don't know."

Again Megan asked, "Do we tell the others?"

"Yes, I think we should. I don't think he will be back but you never know."

Both women looked to the front of the store to see if anyone was on the sidewalk.

"I was so busy today. How did he pick a time that no one was here?" That concerned Liz and Megan. "Was he watching the mercantile?"

"I will talk to Grandpa when I go home and see what he thinks. Be watchful. I will check back in a little while."

Megan teased her sister, "tomorrow you bring your own lunch."

Megan then turned to leave and went out the backdoor as if nothing had happened.

Liz was glad that Megan was fine. She checked both revolvers again and walked to the front with her broom. She could scout out the street while she was sweeping the front boardwalk. Hopefully those strange men had moved on and Thomas would be coming back anytime.

Megan went to the house and told Luke and her grandfather to come to the porch for a drink. She went inside and prepared a pitcher of well water with cheese and apples. Luke, anxious for a snack, held the door open and waited for her to come out. Abby and Emma had joined them as well. Megan told the story in detail, not leaving out any of it. Lucas stood and walked away for a moment when she got to the part about the backroom. Luke understood the insinuation and ran his fingers through his hair. He didn't like the idea and watched his grandfather, expecting him to take to his horse and gun.

He turned back to his family on the porch and said, "This bothers me. I don't think he was after the records. Has any one of you mentioned the gold?"

They all looked to each other and then to Grandpa Mailly and shook their heads no.

Megan asked, "Do you know anything about Tex, Thomas or the others? When will they return?"

"Expecting them any day, but in the mean time, start packing your gun. Luke, that means you too."

Luke knew this was a serious event, but he was still excited to carry a gun and be living in the wild west. "Aunt Megan seemed fine and his mother was a strong woman. She could handle most anything," he thought.

"Luke, I'm going over to see your mother. Start nailing those boards up on the north wall and I'll be right there."

Lucas walked around to the side of the mercantile. He could hear the sweeping of the broom before he could see her. The swishing sound had an even stroke and did not appear to be distressed. This calmed him some. When he reached the end of the boardwalk, he could see her. Liz was sweeping but her eyes were scanning the street, searching for any useful information. His boots made a loud whack when he stepped up on the boardwalk a little too forceful. Liz jumped and let out a small gasp.

"Grandpa! You about scared the life out of me," she exclaimed holding the broom handle like a weapon.

Lucas put his hands up to surrender. "I'm sorry," he chuckled, "didn't mean to frighten you. Heard you two already had a scare." Lucas placed a hand on his granddaughter's shoulder and looked her in the eyes. "When you leave tonight, I will come over and help you lock up. We don't need to be taking any chances. The others will be around soon and we will see what Tex has to say. Seems they already had the acquaintance of the Rangers. Tex will know if they are trouble or not. Think I'll talk to Parker about some sort of nightly guard duty until we find a few things out."

Liz listened and understood, shaking her head in agreement. She started to sweep the top step, thinking that her grandfather was finished.

Lucas paused, "heard I got one granddaughter married off today."

Liz stopped sweeping, remembering what Megan had said earlier. "How does it look for the other one?"

Liz sat on the step with a bewildered look. "I don't know. I seem to have a continuous problem with Thomas. I don't mean to cause him so much pain. He just expects me to do it his way. He is so good to me, sweet and kind. But, then, he just has an opinion about it all. The only way we can get along is for me to keep my mouth shut." Liz sat quiet, knowing that would never work.

Her grandfather was now sitting by her and chuckled. "Liz, you're both adults, you will find a way. Marry Thomas and have fun figuring it out. Don't waste precious time. Everyday is a gift from God, you know that. I wish I had one more day with Claire." He was quiet for a moment. He knew that Liz wished that about Caleb too. "Do you care for Thomas?"

"Yes, when he rode away and didn't see the quilt, I knew that I cared."

"Marry the man, as soon as he returns."

Lucas gave her shoulder a hug and he stood to go.

"See you at closing."

Liz loved her grandfather and was thankful that she had him for so many years. Her best times were with him on a porch, figuring out life. She would remember every piece of advice that he had given her while sitting out on the steps of the old porch back in Riverton..

Chapter Thirteen

Each Day Is a Gift

Liz continued to have a busy afternoon. The day passed quickly and she was grateful for that. It was a good deterrent to help forget the lunch encounter and soon she forgot to be frightened. Each time the bell on the door jingled with a customer Liz gladly looked up to see who it was and now the evening was upon her. She pulled a wooden stool up to the register counter, the same one that Megan had found refuge on earlier that day. Liz went though each transaction and entered them on the page. She drew a line at the bottom of the sheet as she completed the final bookkeeping in her ledger. It had been their most prosperous day so far. The order book had three pages of supplies to order. A smiled formed on her lips as she thought back to Fanny's new stove and how proud her husband was to order it for his wife. Liz enjoyed being a part of the secret. She was thrilled that the business was off to a good start and that her grandfather's dreams were a reality. Texas would be a place that the family could take root.

Liz looked to the back door wondering when her grandfather would be back. She wanted to tell him about the sales for the day and find out about the next freight wagon. She flipped the pencil back and forth in her slender fingers.

The sun was shining in the side window which meant the work day was over and she needed to be through with her accounting. The ledger was closed and placed below the shelf next to her pistol. A copper colored bag with a drawstring at the top was where the day's proceeds were always put and taken to a safe holding place. Lucas really needed to build a vault as a bank was not within a week's ride. She tossed the bag full of coins and bills next to the ledger and the gun as she realized that the front door was still unlocked. The clock chimed and Liz expected Lucas at any moment. Her view of the house out back was obstructed from where she stood and if her grandfather was coming across the way, it was unknown to her. Confidently she went to the front to bolt the red doors.

Just as she went to click the lock, the two filthy men from earlier pushed in through the door and pointed a long gun barrel in her ribs. Liz fell backwards and landed on a pickle barrel. The skinny man who had stood out front grabbed her by the chin with one hand and squeezed her face so hard that her teeth cut into her cheek. She could barely breathe.

"Where is the money?" he growled at her as he leaned down applying more pressure. His breath was on her face and she could not even turn her head to get away from the odor. The tall thin man squeezed harder and shook her head as if that would give him the answer that he was after.

The larger one who had bought bullets from Megan kicked the door shut and came closer.

"This one is different," he said, bearing down upon her with his bloodshot eyes.

The way he looked at Liz made her feel as if she had no clothing on. It sent shivers down her back. She felt truly frightened, maybe for the first time in her life.

He waved his gun at Liz and pulled on her dress sleeve, ripping it and baring one shoulder.

Liz could smell his filth and realized that the skinny one had turned loose of her face, it was numb. Her breathing was labored as she rubbed her cheek, willing the pain to go away as she tasted blood in her mouth. Without being noticed she started to move backwards and get some space between her and the danger at hand. But only for a moment, as now the big one had her by the neck and her toes were the only thing touching the ground.

He growled at her as her held her against a support post. "You can make this fun and give us what we want or we just do it our way." His stare went from her face to her bare shoulder and he licked it, his eyes watching her face. His dirty calloused hand held her firmly around the neck, causing her air flow to be blocked. Liz was only somewhat aware that he had touched her shoulder with his nasty mouth, but her stomach turned.

Without much air, Liz was getting foggy and it was hard to focus. She knew that she was in a desperate situation and that it had nothing to do with the county records. She must fight and she prayed for help. "God, please help me!"

The big man loosened his grip slightly and she took a gulp of much needed air. Her brain cleared enough that she could think and she reached under her apron for the gun. He stood just a step away from her and was unaware of her movements.

The skinny man looked to the red doors and reached to turn the lock. He came closer to her and repeated, "Where is the money?"

Liz thought that he looked more evil than anything she had ever seen before. It was clear that they would kill her. Liz's fingers found the gun under the apron and she pointed it at the big man's gut and squeezed the trigger. The colt went off and both men looked at her not knowing where it had come from. Then the big man loosened his grip and fell to the floor pushing Liz down with him.

There was a hole in Liz's apron and blood was splattered across her. She fumbled to get up, knowing that she would have to pull the trigger once again. The blood on her face was not of concern to her or that the man lying across her was most likely dead.

The skinny man was not looking at Liz or the dead man on the floor, but at the back of the store. He was determined to get the money.

She knew that he would try to get the proceeds of the day and kill her too. He knocked over the display she had made earlier that day and buttons went flying across the floor like an ant hill that had been disturbed. Just as he reached the register two gun shots went off.

Liz got to her knees and saw two men on the wooden floor of the mercantile covered in blood. In disbelief, she realized her beloved grandfather, with a gun in his hand, was lying in a pool of his own blood. She scrambled across the floor toward her grandfather, looking for the gun of the intruder as she crawled. Liz stayed low in case more gun fire was headed her way. Finally, she saw the gun of the tall man and slid it under the denim display. He was not moving.

"Oh God, there is a lot of blood," Liz thought, "this can't be happening, surely it isn't real."

Tears were streaming down her face; she was unaware when they started. Still crawling on her hands and knees, she reached her beloved Grandpa. She was choking on the flood of tears as she reached for his face, not knowing where to touch him.

Lucas opened his eyes and winced in pain. He lifted his head a little, taking in the new calm. "Are they dead?" he asked and laid his head back down.

Liz looked back at the two men and said, "I think so." She could only make out images through her tears.

Liz took the hem of her petticoat and ripped a section off with her teeth. She quickly folded it and looked for the location of the blood. There was so much crimson everywhere she had a hard time finding the source of it all. Lucas moaned when she did and applied pressure to his left chest area.

"Don't leave me!" Liz demanded and wiped at her face with the edge of her dress. "We will get you some help! It will be here any moment. Just stay with me." Liz tried to gain a little control. The blood continued to fill the petticoat bandage.

Lucas' voice was weak as he spoke.

"Liz, take care of the others. Remember where your strength comes from."

Liz didn't want to think about her beloved grandfather dying, but he was.

"Please, please don't go," Liz sobbed leaning down to him, her dress soaking up his life blood. Her arms were around his thick neck and her body across his chest.

He stuttered out his last words, "Liz, the death angel is here for me. I see him in his white robe and the pearly gates are behind him," he coughed and more blood was coming from his mouth, his words slurred, "marry Thomas, each day is a gift."

His eyes began to shut and he whispered, "I hear the glorious music, the gates are so tall, they really are made from one pearl, they never shut. My beautiful Claire is waiting for me there."

Elizabeth Bromont was completely limp and lying on her grandfather. She could hear his heart trying to pump blood that was no longer there. She felt his last breath as it escaped his body. She didn't even hear her own cries. Liz only felt the pain in her own heart. This was pain that she had felt before.

Chapter Fourteen

Home Again

The sun had started to hang low and the riders were anxious to be home. Thomas, Tex and Samuel had ridden together for two days. They didn't talk much but Thomas began to like Samuel a little more. He learned that Samuel and Anna were siblings and that Smithy was their paw. They were an upstanding part of the community and Samuel owned land for a ranch not far from the land Thomas had filed on.

The swaying motion of the horses as they walked hypnotized Thomas and took him deep into his own thinking.

Thomas thought back to the land office in Houston.

The door jingled as he entered and the man with round glasses peered up from his desk.

"Be right with you mister," he said and adjusted the bill of his hat.

Thomas watched the little man as he continued with his project and dipped his pen into the inkwell three more times before looking up at Thomas again.

"Welcome to the Texas Land Office. What county are you filing in?"

The man had his spectacles on the end of his long, pointed nose. He resembled a rat. He looked over the top of them at Thomas.

"Denton County," Thomas responded.

The man pulled out a new form and dipped his pen. He held it firmly and proceeded to fill in the lines. Within an hour, Thomas had filed on his land.

"I need to send a letter, can I borrow a paper and pen?" Thomas asked the clerk.

The man reached into his desk and pulled out a clean sheet and pen with an inkwell. "You can write over there," he motioned to a counter by a window.

Thomas looked out to a busy city. Horses and people were all in a hurry to go somewhere. He thought the quiet countryside that he had purchased was just what he wanted. He would not miss the hum of city life.

He looked forward to sharing his excitement with Liz, Lucas and the family.

Thomas picked up his pen and began to write:

Found land to purchase in Denton County. It is north of where we are at now. Ready for the total amount. Send it with the next freight wagon leaving Saint Louis. Also please arrange for my inheritance and all items to be shipped as soon as possible. Thanks, your nephew Thomas W. Bratcher.

Thomas read the letter over again and folded it to go into the envelope. He addressed the outside and sealed it closed.

"Where can I post this letter?

"Down the street a ways." The clerk motioned to the west with an ink stained finger. He rubbed his nose and now it had ink on it.

Thomas chuckled with the image.

Samuel asked Tex a question and woke Thomas from his past.

"We will be in Worth within the hour," Tex answered.

Thomas was beginning to recognize the countryside and he enjoyed the landscape. His own land looked much like this. He was fast becoming a Texan in the way he thought and rode. He thought about his plans of breeding fine horses and cattle and where exactly he would place the house. Did he want it to face the west or east? He even pondered where Liz would want to put the hen house. It was easy to think on the back of a horse with its gentle sway as it walked along.

He reminded himself to give Abby some news. Thomas had found out about the permanent school fund of 1854. Abby would have some grant money for her school. Thomas had the paperwork for it in his saddle bag. It had been a very good trip to Houston.

Tex stopped his horse for a moment. "I think that's gunfire!"

The three riders jabbed their spurs at the flanks of their mounts, leaned close to their mares and rode hard toward Fort Worth.

Chapter Fifteen

Gone

As Thomas, Tex and Samuel rode onto the dirt streets of Fort Worth, they saw some activity out front of the mercantile. Horses stood silently without riders and a few people that Thomas had not met turned to look at him strangely. Thomas could not put his finger on what it was. The crowd watched as the three began to quickly dismount and tie up their horses.

Tex pulled his gun and cautiously looked around, not sure of the circumstances. Gunpowder hung in the air as well as the smell of death.

The red doors swung open and Pastor Parker came out with a hollow look. He didn't smile or come over to shake their hands and welcome their return.

This was the part Pastor Parker disliked the most, informing the family of a death. "We don't need that now," Parker said motioning to the guns that all three men had pulled from their holsters.

Thomas had taken the steps of the mercantile three at a time and was now standing with Parker. Thomas went for the front door as Parker placed his hand on his shoulder.

"Liz is inside, she needs you. Lucas is gone."

Thomas shoved through the doors and looked for Liz. He stepped over a dead man. He had to walk a ways to see Liz crumpled on the floor with her grandfather. She was rocking back and forth sobbing with no sound. Only the occasional gasp of breath was on her lips as her shoulders shook. Blood was all over Liz. He couldn't tell if any of it was hers or not.

Megan was on her knees at her grandfather's head, with one arm on Liz's shoulder and the other under Lucas' neck, weeping quietly. Abby and Emma stood by the backdoor of the mercantile quietly in shock, tears streaming down their face. Abby held the edge of her apron and used it to stop the tears at her chin. A thick trail of blood trickled past them on the wood floor and dripped at the back step.

Young Luke was a short distance away in the yard. He stood like a fence post. His hands were jammed down in his pockets and he was ashen in color. Luke kicked at a rock and took off running to the woods by the Cavalry barracks. Luke knew well the pain in his chest. He wanted to handle his feelings alone in the woods. There he didn't have to worry about being a man. The little boy could cry out at the injustice of losing a grandfather and a father so close together.

Thomas saw his mentor, a man he loved and respected, lying on the crimson stained wooden floor. He looked to his left at the register and saw another dead man, unknown to him with the copper colored register bag lying open on the floor next to him. A few coins had fallen out. It now became clear to him that the men had tried to rob the mercantile. Thomas looked back to Liz and saw the torn dress.

"What else did they try?" Thomas thought and anger began to rise up in him.

Thomas bent his long legs and reached for Liz. She was unaware that he was even there. Thomas helped her stand and she became limp in his arms. She had no words, her throat couldn't move and her nose burned. She buried her face into his chest. She was covered in blood. Her face was splattered and her hands looked painted. Her dress was soaked by her grandfather's blood as she kneeled next to him.

Thomas reached out for Megan and the two Wilkes who hovered at the back entry. This was his family and he had a lot of comforting to do. He would tend to his own grief later. He gathered them into his arms, smoothed their hair and spoke gently to the four women as the tears continued to fall.

Tex now came to the group and offered his sympathy to the Mailly family.

Thomas looked to Tex and said. "Has anyone seen Luke? Does he know?" Thomas never released his arms from the women as he spoke.

"I'll see what I can find out," Tex nodded his head and walked to the door. Parker and Samuel listened to Tex and then went out the door and turned left to go find Luke.

Thomas spoke softly to his group of women. He knew that they needed to get to the house and get some sleep. Sleep was the best thing right now. "Do you think we can go to the house and get Liz in some different clothing, Megan too?"

Abby looked up and was ready to get her mind on a task. She was also inclined to leave this place and never come back. She took one last look over to her grandfather and asked, "Thomas, can we go out the front door?"

Thomas led Liz and Megan to the front. Abby held her sister's hand as they passed by the first dead intruder. Emma stopped for a moment and spit on him as she began to move away. Abby saw her sister and didn't say one word to her.

A group of people had gathered on the street in the evening sun.

The women dabbed at their eyes and the men held their hats in their hands. One small boy hid in his mother's skirt. Liz saw all of this in slow motion as Thomas took her home.

They were at the backdoor of the small porch when Thomas saw the quilt on the chair. Megan was watching Thomas as he noticed it. His mind went back to the morning that he had ridden out.

Thomas looked over to Megan and asked, "Has it been there the whole time?"

Megan just shook her head silently and held the door open for the rest of them. She saw a look of new sadness come over Thomas and placed her hand on his shoulder as he went by her.

Inside, Emma started the tea kettle while Abby went with Liz and Megan to help with the clothing.

Anna came to the door. "Thomas, I will see about things here. I'm prepared to stay the night. Parker and Tex could use your help at the store. Samuel found Luke and he is bringing him back here in a while." Anna looked at Thomas with sympathy and gave him a hug. "Thomas there was nothing you could do, even if you had been here. We don't know why bad things happen to good people. But, God is good and he will get us through this tragedy," Anna smiled and turned to go to help the others.

Thomas stood on the back porch in the new darkness. His chest felt as if the weight of the world was upon it. He had let this family down. If only he had been here and not gone again. Thomas hung his head and took a breath deep enough to make his chest heave. As he started to the mercantile he saw the quilt again.

"Where had it been the morning he rode away? How did he miss it? Would it have kept him here? Could he have saved Lucas?" The questions made his already pounding head swim as he went to help move the dead.

The breakfast table was mostly silent when Tex tapped at the door. Anna opened it and welcomed Samuel inside as well. She poured steaming cups of coffee and set them before them. Thomas had now appeared and poured his own. He leaned on the cupboard as Tex began to talk.

"We know these two outlaws who were at the mercantile. We suspect them in two other robberies and three murders. Never thought that they would be put down by a woman and her grandfather," Tex paused for a moment before he continued. He looked away holding back any emotion. He tapped his boot and clicked his mouth as he got out. "Real sorry for the loss of your grandfather. I enjoyed working with him. He thought highly of all of you," Tex smiled as he thought back, "I thought for the longest that he had all sons, would have never known from the way he spoke of you that you would have been women."

Samuel spoke next. "Parker and Smithy have Lucas at the church," Samuel swallowed and pushed the lump down in his throat, "he looks real peaceful."

Liz swiped at the continual stream of tears that flowed silently. Abby handed her a fresh hanky with an embroidered A on the corner.

"We plan to have a prayer service at the church then the burial. Will that be fine?" Samuel asked soberly.

"Thank you Samuel," Megan replied, "We will be ready."

A few gray clouds slumbered across the sky as Lucas Mailly's friends and family stood by the open grave. Lucas had not been in Texas long but the people had already come to care about this new family. The men held their hats in their hands and the women dabbed at their faces with hankies. They were smaller in number than what gathered at Caleb's grave side but sincere with their sorrow.

Pastor Parker began with these words. "Praise be to God and Father of our Lord Jesus Christ, the Father of compassion and the God of all comfort, who comforts us in all trouble, so that he we can comfort those in need. Blessed are those who mourn, for they shall be comforted. He will wipe away all sorrow, crying and pain." Parker paused for a moment and cleared his throat from the huskiness. "If you have a relationship with Jesus, you will see Lucas again, rejoice in that. If you do not, you have a real reason to mourn, for you will never see Lucas Mailly again."

Liz remembered the face of her grandfather. He was lying in the wooden box wrapped in the last quilt that his beloved Claire had made for him. Granny had used browns and golds to make the border of trees and the forest. Lucas did look nice in his Sunday clothing. She was glad that Megan suggested the timber trail quilt as a burial cloth.

Sweet Anna Parker began to sing, "When we all get to Heaven."

The crowd looked up at her as she sang the uplifting song. A few heads motioned in agreement.

Liz thought that she had just begun to become normal from the unexpected drowning of her husband and now she was becoming numbed again to the world around her. She had no desire to enter the world of the living dead again. She bowed her head to pray. "God, I can't do this again. I don't want to put up a wall around my heart. Please, sweep me away in your love and comfort. I can't do this alone."

Liz was silent with her head lowered and she heard her answer dropped into her soul, clear as a bell. "You are not alone, I am here in your sadness. I will carry you and comfort you. Do not put on a brave face, come to me in your pain. I am as close as your breath and I love you."

Liz knew that voice. She was always amazed how God could talk to her so personally. She whispered, "Thank you God, I love you too."

She raised her head and took a small step closer to Thomas. Her gloved hand found his hand and she wrapped her fingers into his. Thomas looked down to her and she smiled weakly. Elizabeth Mailly looked over the crowd of people, some she did not know at all but they were there for her family. She began to pray a silent pray of thanksgiving for them all. Liz could feel the strength coming back to her and she took a breath of hope.

She would be strong and comfort her family through this tragedy. She knew how to do it, she had done it before.

After the burial Parker came over to Liz and gave her a white cloth. It was custom in the South to save a lock of hair of the deceased. Liz unfolded it and saw the thick gray curl of her grandfather.

"Thank you Parker. I will place it in the family Bible."

Chapter Sixteen
The Best of Times

Thomas and Liz had been sitting on the porch for hours. The crispness that comes with fall was not in the air yet but the evening was pleasant. They had cried and laughed together as they talked out the issues that gave their relationship grief.

Thomas looked upon Liz with admiration. It had only been a few weeks since the passing of Lucas and she was smiling. He was amazed by her strength and focus.

Liz reached down and picked up Cally, the half grown kitten from her Riverton home. John and Blue had brought it back with them when they returned with the latest freight wagons. Cally had been sleeping on the porch with Luke's dog, Bear. Emma had been concerned that the cat would be eaten by coyotes that prowled the night. Their prairie song could be heard several nights during the week and it sent shivers through the young woman.

"Thank you for asking Blue to bring Cally to us. We all do enjoy her and it is a little like home." Liz paused and stroked the soft yellow fur.

"Thomas, I think we should set a date to be married. We don't need to wait any longer. I would like to have the wedding at the church with Parker and the rest of our friends and family with one of those great street dances. You know like we had at Fort Polk and here when we first arrived. Will you still have me?" she teased.

Thomas stopped rocking and leaned over to place his elbows on his knees. He then reached out and took both of her hands. "Liz, I think that is a wonderful idea; I will talk to Parker right away."

Abby and Samuel had just ridden up from making some school calls from farther away. Abby had contacted almost all of the families personally. The ones she made today were from a distance and difficult to find in the heavy growth of the trees. She did not have many roads to follow, only trails. Samuel knew the area and had insisted that he ride with her. Abby had complained that it was not proper for her to be alone with him. Samuel just made Abby complain more when he informed her that she would have to ride a horse astride or they would not be able to cover the required distance. She finally gave in when he suggested that it would be an overnight trip otherwise.

"Abby, I'm a school board member. It is my responsibility to assist you." Samuel persisted until Abby gave in.

"Miss Abby packed us a delicious lunch and we had a successful day," Samuel told Thomas and Liz as he stepped down from his horse. He gave his horse a pat and tossed the reins over the post. Abby swiped at some trail dust on her sleeve and noticed the grins on Thomas and Liz.

"You two look…" The school teacher paused as she thought about catching students in the act of mischief. "What did we miss out on today?"

Samuel now had both horses tethered and reached up to help the school marm from her horse. Abby placed her hands on his shoulders to keep a proper distance when he reached out for her waist and swung her down. Abby planted her feet on the ground and gave Samuel the disapproving teacher look.

Thomas and Liz both were standing on the porch watching the proper teacher and the lawyer. Thomas stepped off the porch happy to see that Samuel had his eye on someone other than his Liz. Thomas had suspected weeks ago that Samuel was sweet on Abby. Samuel had become a good friend and Thomas wanted him to be happy as well. They would be neighbors someday. It was easier to be friends.

"The day went well?" Liz asked.

"It was good," Abby replied, "I only have a few more families to visit and we will be ready for the school year to begin. I have the twelve required to get the assistance from the state. Thank you again, Thomas, for help with that. It would have taken so long to get any funding from back East. I do have some school supplies coming on the next freight wagon."

"What have you two been up to today? My teacher instinct tells me you have a secret," Abby quipped as she stepped to the porch.

Thomas looked to Liz for her approval and she smiled back with a nod. "Liz and I are ready to celebrate a wedding."

"That is wonderful," Abby rejoiced and gave her cousin a hug.

Samuel shook Thomas' hand and winked at Liz. She smiled back at his good humored teasing. She placed her hand inside of Thomas' and gave a little squeeze.

Megan, Emma and Anna were just coming around from the garden with baskets and aprons full of a garden harvest. They set their abundance on the porch with excitement.

"It will be a busy few days with all of this needing to be canned. Anyone want to join us?" Megan asked looking about the group of women. Knowing well that Liz would be at the mercantile and Abby was in full swing of school starting.

Samuel's mouth started watering at the image of fresh baked pies and buttery ears of corn. "I am more than able and not ashamed to wash any dishes in return for a dinner invitation."

Laughter was heard around the circle of friends. Liz looked at the group and realized what a wonderful group of friends and family she had. It was good to be in Fort Worth. Her Grandpa Lucas was right. She hoped that she would be able to have the wisdom that Lucas had possessed. She also suspected that several of these friends would turn into family.

"Lucas would be proud," she thought. "They were all healing well. The best of times were just ahead and she would see to it that they did not get away."

They were interrupted by one of Liz's roosters coming around the corner with feathers flying and the most unusual racket. The bird's feet were barely touching the ground. Luke and his dog, Bear, came around to the porch looking sheepish.

"Maybe that could be a chicken dinner invitation," Samuel laughed.

Chapter Seventeen
Little Dove

A bby was in her schoolroom putting the finishing touch on a few projects. She was placing her plaid basket quilt on the wall. It was a great way to teach the girls some math. It had always worked well in the past. The plaid with the little berries on it was her favorite piece of fabric. Her mother had a large scrap of it from one of her dresses and she was able to use it for the border. This quilt was sewn when she was almost grown and it brought back sweet memories of her youth.

Abby heard the door swing open and she turned to walk back and shut it, thinking that the wind had been the culprit. She was surprised to see a young Indian girl with shining black hair standing in the doorway. Abby shocked at the sight, placed her hand to her chest and shut her mouth which had fallen open.

"I'm Little Dove." She spoke amazing well and came a few steps closer. Her skirt jingled with some type of beads that she had on a leather string around her waist. Abby saw that the skirt was made of soft animal skins and her shirt was of cotton. Little Dove had long dark lashes and jet black eyes which looked confident.

"Are you the new teacher?" Little Dove looked expectantly at Abby who was still speechless.

"Yes. Yes, I am Miss Abigail Wilkes the new teacher here in Fort Worth. How did you know about the classes starting?"

Abby resumed her composure and had several questions of her own for the young woman. Little Dove gave her story with no emotion.

"My mother married a white man and we lived in the hills with her people, the Apaches, until the soldiers came. I learned both tongues. My father was killed and we were sold as slaves. Passed around by thieves and outlaws mostly." The Indian girl dropped a quilt that was beautifully pieced on the desk and started the story again.

"Ma died awhile back and the men stayed away from me if I kept the food plentiful and hid out."

Abby stepped closer still unaware of what part of the story she would play. She nodded her head for her to continue.

Little Dove licked her lips and lowered her dark lashes. "The lawless men who held me captive are the two men that killed your family."

Abby's mouth fell open again as she thought of those two wicked men and this young girl enslaved to them. She was clean and neat in her appearance. She had no smell. Abby could not even form the next question, so the girl continued again.

"Tex found me when the Rangers come to the camp and told me that they were dead. He said I should be in Miss Abby's classroom."

Little Dove went to her quilt with the pumpkin colored border and black check. She unfolded it and it held all of her belongings.

"Tex said that he wished that he could be in your classroom and that I should not waste any time." She sat at the desk ready for her first lesson.

"Tex burned the place it was so filthy. This was all he let me take."

Abby just stood taking it all in. Finally she formed some words.

"This is a lovely quilt. Did you make it?" Abby came close enough to touch the softness of the scraps.

"My mother made it for me. She said it was not woven like an Indian blanket but that she could use the same design. I do know how to sew," she said matter of factly.

Abby remembered back to the fire that took the life of Liz and Megan's parents. The two little girls were found with only an appliquéd quilt. Abby smiled at Little Dove and placed her hand on her shoulder.

"I would love to have you in class when we start in a few days. Your English is very good. I think you will be an excellent student. Did you walk here?"

She shook her head yes as she looked at her pretty new teacher. "Three days, I slept three nights in the trees."

"Oh," Abby was surprised. "Why in a tree?"

"I don't have to worry over the night animals finding me."

"Oh," Abby said again.

"Let's see if we can find you a place to sleep that will be a little more comfortable. My house is a little full at the present time. I want you to met my find Anna, let's go find her."

Little Dove gathered her quilt of belongings and stood to follow Abby out the door and down the steps to the unknown. She seemed unafraid to sleep at a stranger's home. Abby waited at the door for her new charge. She chatted as they went to knock on Anna's door.

Anna welcomed the two and asked them in for tea. She listened intently to the story and asked a few questions of her own. Little Dove seemed unharmed by the violence in her young life. She was pretty, well mannered and her spoken word was better than many of her classmates would be.

"My husband, Parker, and I would enjoy your young company. We would be happy for you to stay as long as you would like. And I'm close to the school," Anna teased as she was right next door.

"Come this way and I will show you your room." Anna motioned to her new bedroom.

Little Dove couldn't believe her good fortune. Tex was right these were good people who would look after her. She placed her quilt bundle on the bed and set down looking it over.

Anna stood in the sitting room and said to Abby quietly, "Do you think those dirty outlaws left her alone?"

"Hopefully they did. She said that she cooked and stayed out of their way. She is so young, maybe they saw her as a child, even unsociable because she is Indian," Abby stated.

Anna smiled and looked at the girl. She finally had a child in her home.

Chapter Eighteen

Celebration

L iz stood and ran her hands down the front of her borrowed wedding dress to smooth out any wrinkles. Anna was a dear to let her use the one that her mother had made for her own vows with Parker. Megan had worked on it for three days to make it fit just perfectly. The shoulders of the dress rested just across the tips of Liz's own shoulders. Her skin was smooth and creamy next to the princess cut neckline. Liz took a deep breath and bit the edge of her lip. She wasn't use to wearing such a low neckline.

"I could never get a full day's worth of work done in this." Liz twisted her shoulders in the elegant white gown. Her hands rested on her slim waist.

Anna stood with her at the back of the church. "You look beautiful. Now be still or you will fall out of that dress," Anna teased and checked Liz's hair in the back.

"There is no way that this dress could fall off of me," Liz thought. It fits me so snugly."

"Are you ready? Thomas is at the front waiting for you and he looks so handsome."

Liz took a step and could see down the short aisle. Thomas stood at the front and he was handsome. But, what made her heart skip a beat was his character. She saw a man stable, strong and sure of himself. His persona made him more than just a good-looking man. She would enjoy persuading him to see things her way. Lucas was right. They would have fun working it all out.

Thomas wore a crisp white button down shirt and a black string tie. It fit him neatly across his shoulders. He looked natural and at ease in his western wear. His hands were fidgety, not knowing what to do. He twisted a small sterling ring at the tip of his little finger. This was the ring that he had bought from the peddler for Liz. When Liz stepped into the aisle where he could see her, she took his breath away for a moment. She would be his wife.

Luke stood next to Thomas and he smiled at them both. When Liz reached the alter Thomas took her hand and they both turned to stand before Pastor Parker.

Liz was truly happy. She thought that she would never marry again when Caleb passed on so tragically. She did care for Thomas in a new and exciting way. Life was meant for the living and it was so much better when two shared the harness. Elizabeth Bratcher would be her new name. She would always be a Mailly even though it was a name she never carried.

Megan wore a blue dress that she had made special for the wedding and stood at her sister's side. She looked at Liz and a tear slid down her cheek. Both sisters carried a wildflower bouquet of yellow sunflowers and black-eyed susans.

Abby pulled out one of her embroidered hankies and dabbed at one eye as she looked at the bridal party. She passed a fresh hanky to her sister who sniffled next to her.

The church was full of family and friends who had come for the

124

wedding, dinner and dance. Tex and the Rangers were there dressed in their good clothes. Jackson and Colt cleaned up well and it was good to have them home for a while.

Parker talked of love and patience and forgiveness. He gave good words to live by. He finished quickly and asked the congregation to meet Thomas and Elizabeth Bratcher. Thomas grinned from ear to ear and swept his bride up in a kiss. The crowd clapped and whooped as he pulled her down the aisle to the doors of the church.

Liz had not eaten much during the day and now that the ceremony was complete she was famished. The food couldn't be ready soon enough.

"Thomas, I could eat a whole chicken!" Liz exclaimed.

Thomas thought his bride looked beautiful and had a hard time realizing that this day was real. Liz was happy and that was a big comfort to him. The day went perfectly and he wanted to dance with her as soon as he could get her away from the food.

The music was imploring and lively and the dance floor filled up quickly with couples. The fiddle played a Virginia reel.

Jackson was quick to take Megan out in the midst of dancers. They whirled around Samuel and Abby who were already in step.

Colt looked around and found Emma at the chocolate cake. She took his hand and he spun her in a circle as the music picked up.

Luke put his youthful shyness aside and asked Little Dove to take the dance floor with him. She agreed and seemed to be able to follow. Her black hair reflected blue with the light. She was fitting in well already. Luke liked the jingle her belt made as they stepped it out.

Tex stood with Smithy and thought how Lucas should be there watching his family celebrate. He would be proud of them. As Tex watched the couples, he wondered how long it would be before the next wedding in north Texas.

JODI BARROWS is a nationally known quilting teacher, speaker and writer. She currently lives in the North Texas area. Over the past twenty years, Jodi has remarkably touched thousands of quilters throughout the world with her unique method called Square in a Square®. Her point of view provides the quilter with the freedom to create most any quilt design with speed and accuracy.

Jodi has spoken to quilting audiences throughout the United States, Canada, and Australia. She has appeared as a guest on several quilting shows, including TNN's Aleene's Creative Living, TNN's Your Home Studio, Perfecting Patchwork on Family Net TV, and PBS series with Kaye Wood. HGTV has shown her commercial on the quilting techniques she has developed on the Simply Quilts show.

The Square in a Square® system is a process that anyone can implement in most any design. Jodi has written sixteen books (ten of which have been on the best seller's list), two novels, produced four tools, two video/DVDs and five teacher's books. Additionally, she has a pattern book and fabric line based on a fiction novel she wrote from the 1856 time period entitled "Leaving Riverton."

She also has a Certified Teacher's Program in the United States and Canada. Jodi has had numerous quilts appear in McCall's, The Quilter, Quick and Easy Quilt World, House of White Birch Publications, Quilter's Newsletter Top Ten New Products, Leisure Arts Scrappy Bed Quilts 2003, Round Bobbin Quilting Professional, and a Featured Teacher in the Traditional Quilter.

Jodi has been commissioned to compose quilts for many state and national organizations as well as working with the Kansas Historical Society. She has been active in guilds as well as owning several crafting and sewing related businesses over the years. Jodi was raised in southwest Kansas, has 2 grown sons, and is married to Steve, her high school sweetheart.

*S*NS
PUBLISHING

Square In A Square • 1613 Lost Lake Drive • Keller, Texas 76248

TOLL FREE 1-888-624-6260 FAX 817-605-7420 EMAIL snsjodi@yahoo.com • WEB www.SquareInASquare.com

Abby's schoolhouse sample chapter

Abby was bent over and had her back to the students. She was placing more wood into the stove that heated the classroom. Samuel was in charge of school maintenance. He had put some of the older boys in charge of cutting the wood and stacking it neatly for Abby. Abby thought it was good of Samuel to always be checking on her and the students.

At first she thought that they did not trust her. But now, she saw it as care and responsibility to the education of the students. The community was excited about the school.

A cold front had unexpectedly come through and Abby rubbed her hands together to warm them as well as dust them. The wind started to howl and rain drops hit the window.

As Abby turned to face her pupils, the door burst open. The storm had brought more than a change in the weather. Three masked gunmen faced Abby and her students.

Samuel had been out to his ranch for several days. His mind kept going back to every meeting and conversation with the new school marm. He just couldn't keep her off of his mind. He enjoyed teasing her. She was so proper it wasn't hard to get a reaction from her.

He saw the dark clouds moving in and realized the storm was already over the town. He didn't want to be stuck out at his place for the storm and decided it was a good time to go back. Besides, he needed to check on the school. It was his responsibility anyway.

Homestead Star
75" x 85"

Mrs. Sewell's Star
110" x 110"

131

**Peddler's
Choice**
67" x 75"

Split Bear Paw
73" x 92"

**Monkey
Tails**
63" x 74"

Lickety Split
Anna's Quilt
50" x 60"

Timber Trails
Grandpa's Quilt
63" x 63"

**Abby's Basket
Sampler**
54" x 69"

Indian Blanket
76" x 88"

**Emma's
Crossroads**
89" x 105"